Praise for Maureen Hancock and *The Medium Next Door*

"In *The Medium Next Door*, Maureen Hancock weaves the fabric of everyday life into accounts of communication across different realms—providing the reader with a comfortable and believable platform. Not only is Maureen the 'real deal' when it comes to spirit communication, she is also a grounded individual with great integrity, a caring nature, and a wonderful sense of humor. I was fortunate enough to personally experience a reading with Maureen—conducted under restricted conditions. She shone brightly in this process, as did my smile after receiving unmistakable validations from my beloved son Brandon."

—Mark Ireland, author of *Soul Shift: Finding Where the Dead Go*

"Maureen's ability to interpret and understand messages from the deceased is remarkable. She describes events, locations, and situations so eerily; it's as if she were present when these events occurred. I'm amazed and awestruck at her comprehension and specific knowledge of the lives of people that she's never even met. Her interpretations are inspiring and comforting to the grandest skeptic. A must read for anyone who has lost a loved one and has questions about death, dying, and the continuity of life."

—Cindy Hall Felts, Alamance County Homicide Detective

"Maureen Hancock is the real deal! Maureen's innate ability to connect and receive messages from our loved ones who have passed is truly a divine gift. As a law enforcement officer for thirty years; logic is supported by factual evidence. In 2006, my life changed after her personal reading that was fact driven, connected me to a dear loved one who had passed decades ago; long before the age of computers, internet, and Google. *The Medium Next Door* will open your heart and soul to a new belief that our loved ones really don't die, they are "just different now," as Maureen explains with her connections to Spirit. Her book is full of personal life experiences that are uplifting and comforting, taking away doubt and leaving the reader with strength, hope, and peace."

—John M. LaCross, RI Police Chief
and Retired Major of RI State Police

"When our four-year-old little angel, 'Lulu,' came through Maureen, it was beyond this world! It was beyond any experience I have ever had. Maureen delivers messages with power, humor, and grace. Maureen says that she is clairaudient, but I have witnessed her taking on the complete mannerisms of lost loved ones. Maureen is a gift to the living and the dead! She is the real deal! For anyone who will pass away . . . for anyone who has lost a loved one . . . this book and Maureen are a must-have! If you have ever doubted heaven, doubt no more! Thank you, Maureen, for sharing your gift with the world!"

—Gretchan Pyne, The Lulu Foundation, author of *Lulu's Rose Colored Glasses* and others (visit www.lulubellebooks.com)

The Medium Next Door

Adventures of a Real-Life Ghost Whisperer

Maureen Hancock

Health Communications, Inc.
Deerfield Beach, Florida

www.hcibooks.com

Library of Congress Cataloging-in-Publication Data

Hancock, Maureen.
  The medium next door : the adventures of a real-life ghost whisperer /
Maureen Hancock.
      p. cm.
    ISBN-13: 978-0-7573-1564-0
    ISBN-10: 0-7573-1564-X
    ISBN-13: 978-0-7573-9187-3 (e-book)
    ISBN-10: 0-7573-9187-7 (e-book)
      1. Hancock, Maureen.   2. Mediums—United States—Biography.
  I. Title.
  BF1283.H234A3 2011
  133.9'1092—dc22
  [B]
                                                2011004510

Publisher: Health Communications, Inc.
            3201 S.W. 15th Street
            Deerfield Beach, FL 33442–8190

Cover photo by Kerry Brett of Kerry Brett Lifestyle Portraits
Cover design by Larissa Hise Henoch
Interior design and formatting by Lawna Patterson Oldfield

This book is dedicated to our angel,

Sean Michael Ewas,

who provided the wind beneath my

earthly wings; and to my beautiful family

for their unconditional love

and encouragement.

Contents

Introduction

I'm living a life less ordinary, that's for certain. Let's just say I'm not
your average soccer mom. I should have a walk-in closet just for my
many hats. I start my day like most of the moms in my neighborhood.
After two hits of the snooze button I roll out of bed at 7:20 AM. My
morning beauty routine consists of putting on sweats and sneakers.
I rush downstairs to start breakfast, let Ally, our chocolate lab, out
to make her bladder gladder, and pack snacks, water, and homework.
Then, it's a mad dash to get my two boys, Tyler and Drew, up, fed, and
out the door in time for the eight o'clock school bell. After good-bye
kisses, I go put on my superwoman cloak. You see, I come from a long
line of legendary Irish intuitives and healers. My great-grandmother
had the gift, as did my mother's mother, her sisters, and most especially,
my grandmother's sister, Annie. She was ordered to move to Scotland
by the parish priest of Donegal, Ireland, after he saw dozens of people
camped out in front of her thatched cottage hoping to receive a healing
or reading from her. Mediumship is in my DNA, but it took a couple

of near-death experiences and the tragedy of 9/11 for me to embrace my ability to communicate with those who have passed. Now I share it around the country to help others.

At about 9:00 AM, I arrive at my office in a rural town forty minutes south of Boston, where I meet with my event manager and close friend, Kelly Scriven. Kelly runs through a checklist of things we need to take care of in preparation for a big event or presentation. Next, I check in with my assistant, Wanda, who hands me a to-do list regarding the day's events. Through the Seeds of Hope foundation, I may be scheduled for cancer hands-on-healing work at someone's home or at a hospital. I may also be involved in a search for a missing child or adult through a joint effort with Metro Investigations of Boston. Our organization—Mission for the Missing—provides pro bono services for the missing. In addition, I often meet with parents who have lost a child. I do this to help bring them peace and closure by sharing messages from beyond. Meetings like these often begin with much anguish and crying but usually end with an uplifting transformation and joyful tears and smiles. All my sessions, whether they are a private reading, a cancer-healing visit, or a missing-person case, are free of charge. I'm a firm believer in paying it forward. I believe God blessed me with an ability that I need to share.

By the time the three o'clock school bell rings, I may have assisted the dying, comforted the grieving, solved a mystery, appeared on a radio show, performed a ghostbusting, and located a missing dog—all just in time for hugs, homework, and a hot meal.

"Do we have baseball, soccer, lacrosse, or football tonight?" I ask calmly, as I stir the stew.

After we eat, it's off to the field, where I help coach a game or two. Depending on the day of the week, my next stop may be a Postcards from Heaven event. These gatherings range in size from fifty to five hundred people who are hoping to connect with a loved one who has passed, and take place at a variety of venues, such as restaurants, old Boston theaters, hotels, bookstores, historic inns, and old firehouses. Some Postcards from Heaven events are actually fundraisers to help local charities and families in need.

Known as the "comedian medium," I use humor to take the edge off an overwhelming subject matter: death. After a quick explanation of how I interpret what's coming through from the "other side," I am drawn to various people in the room and give spiritual readings that often involve messages from loved ones in spirit.

In addition to the Postcards from Heaven events, I also teach classes on spirit communication. I especially enjoy teaching people who think it's impossible to speak directly to loved ones in spirit, and I'm overjoyed when I can change their frowns and doubts to smiles and belief. I'm always amazed at the eclectic group of students who show up for these seminars. I've taught doctors, lawyers, judges, FBI agents, state police, nurses, teachers, nonverbal disabled adults, engineers, medical examiners, stay-at-home dads and moms, grandparents, and teens.

But my most precious time is spent with my husband and our two boys in our tiny cape on a dead-end street. When I don't have an event or a class, I love when we gather around the kitchen table for an old-fashioned dinner. Because my schedule is so hectic, I treasure the time I get to spend with my family that much more. The minute my boys get home from school, they ask, "Are you home all day and all night?" It had been the running question for a few years because I was often being called away for an emergency or a family in need. Now, I make it a point to make more time for my family. I believe we all should work to live, not live to work. In my vocation especially, I see how precious every moment is.

At home it's like pulling teeth to find out how school was that day, especially from my nine-year-old. The answer is always the same: "good." Our dinner conversation, however, is a tad different from our neighbors. We might talk about my upcoming events or missing children searches. My boys are very curious about my work. During dinner, they will ask me who I saw that day. Both boys are highly sensitive and compassionate. I will tell them about the sick children I am working with. Their faces show concern and they always ask, "Can we do anything to help those kids?" Drew, my younger son, asks, "Why can't the doctor give the kids medicine to get rid of their cancer?" We talk about how blessed we are and about ways to help others. When dinner is over, one rule is very clear—if I cook, my husband does the dishes. We close out the night with reading a good book aloud before bed.

As for my own family, my mother is a feisty, five-foot-short "head of the God squad" Irishwoman. My dad will greet you with a joke and a smile. I am one of nine children—two boys and seven girls—who shared one bathroom with a claw-foot bathtub. I am the seventh born or the third youngest. Until I was well into my twenties, I was referred to as "one of the three babies."

I count each of my siblings among my treasures. My six sisters and I are a hoot when we go dancing. We are the family of comedians—the popular table at any function. My family has finally gotten used to the fact that "Mo" is a medium. When I first came out, most of my siblings were very accepting. My brother Jim, the psychologist/skeptic, will probably never wrap his brain around what I do. I can tell he's curious but not yet convinced. And what a challenge it was to tell my devout Catholic mother that I was a ghost whisperer. Today, she is my biggest fan and promoter. Dad just sits back and smiles when he hears my stories. When I tell him an old Navy buddy wants to say hi, he just giggles and says, "Oh yeah? Is he still drinking Aqua Velva?" Apparently, any form of alcohol would do when out to sea for months.

Each week of my life brings a new set of challenges and quirky requests: I just got a call about a missing horse. Who loses a horse? Oh, and I have a group of moms who say their children see dead people. And my neighbor lost her diamond. Can I find it?

I'm the freckle-faced girl next door with a twist. I talk to dead people. In addition to daily chats with the deceased, I dedicate my time helping the terminally ill and those family members left behind. I'm a teacher of sorts, demystifying death and celebrating the beautiful transition to the other side. Our physical shell—our body—is a leased vehicle. When the lease is up and the car returned, the driver still exists.

It doesn't matter what our beliefs are, our race is, or how many cars we own. We all have one thing in common: death. We all know someone who has suffered a loss, experienced an illness, or been torn apart by grief.

I have many reasons for writing this book. One is to share information that will help you navigate through the rough waters of life.
Whether you are someone who is cautious but curious, or an optimist
who is in touch with their intuition, or someone in between searching for answers, the techniques I share throughout this book will help
you become more aware and alert when it comes to embracing life or
fine-tuning your inner wisdom. There is peace in knowing that life
continues in spirit once a loved one has passed on.

In these pages I share my life story, the unfolding personal struggles encountered doing mediumship work, and the heartfelt passion
behind my calling to assist the dying. For years I fought my vocation.
Now I can finally say I felt God's gentle nudge. My cup is always half
full, and my heart is bigger than the twenty-four hours in a day. Join
me as I break the mystique of a medium's life by taking you on a journey through this "sixth sense" road of twists and turns.

1

Awakenings

I was born a "veil baby" or a "caulbearer." This simply means that I was born with remnants of the amniotic sac around my head. In days of old, this was considered a sign of good luck. People believed veil babies were gifted with the ability to see the future or to dream things that would come to pass. Some even believed such a child would be able to communicate with the dead.

I'm the seventh of nine children born and raised outside Boston, Massachusetts, in an old white farmhouse. We were seven girls and two boys crammed into four small bedrooms, and we had to battle over one bathroom. I shared a room with my two sisters, Sarah and Patrice. The peeling wallpaper was very seventies—big white daisies on a bright yellow background. Sarah and I reluctantly shared a double bed, and each night I geared up for "the blanket brawl." Because I was smaller, I usually lost.

My dad, Jim Dalton, was a blue-collar worker—a technician for the Boston Gas Company. He serviced commercial stoves in restaurants throughout the city. He always had a funny story to tell and a beer to share, and he'd give you the last two bucks in his pocket if you needed it more than he did. Meanwhile, my mom, Gracie Dalton, stayed at home holding down the fort. In her spare time, she fought for the cause of the week. If there was a wrong to right or a Democrat to be elected, you called my mom. She had a knack for getting things done and done fast. With the old rotary phone receiver wedged between her shoulder and neck, cigarette in one hand, Maxwell House coffee in the other, she went to town organizing volunteers, fighting city hall, and sticking up for the underdog.

From oldest to youngest, my siblings are: Rosie, Jimmy, Liz, Maggie, Joe, Marygrace, Sarah, and Patrice. Each of us has a story to tell, a challenge conquered, and a tragedy triumphed.

As one story goes, when I was about eighteen months old, I'd watch my older siblings play in the yard through the window, being too small to go outdoors with them. My younger sister, Sarah, who was almost a year old, would sit in the playpen next to me. Because I was teething at the time, I would gnaw on the windowsills while I stood there, and this became a habit. What my mother didn't realize was that I was ingesting the paint chips that flaked off the windowsill. Lead-based paint, which has a sweet taste, is very addicting. In fact, this sort of addiction is an actual disorder called pica—the compulsive craving of nonnutritive substances like paper or paint chips. It's more common in young children. Anyway, after a couple of months of my ingesting these paint chips, my mother found me unconscious on the floor of our living room. She picked me up, but I was unresponsive and turning blue, and so she immediately rushed me to Cardinal Cushing Hospital in Brockton, Massachusetts. The doctors were baffled and could not figure out what was wrong with me. My brain began to swell, and I slipped into a coma. Dr. Murphy, our family pediatrician, scoured through medical books well into the night. He finally figured out that I had severe lead-paint poisoning and had me transferred to Children's Hospital in Boston.

Upon arrival at Children's Hospital, a team of surgeons quickly wheeled me into surgery. They placed a brain shunt in my skull to relieve the fluid on my brain (a condition called acute encephalitis). My parents were given the grim news that I would most likely not make it through the night. Unwavering in her faith, my mother took the news standing up. She began a calling crusade, contacting friends, relatives, priests, religious organizations—to put it simply, she called in the God squad. I was put on prayer lists from Boston to Ireland, Italy, and Portugal—everywhere my mother had friends and relatives living.

Their prayers were answered, and I survived the night. But I remained in a coma for two and a half weeks. My parents stayed by my side and took turns sleeping in the chair by my crib. In addition to the brain shunt, needles were inserted in my heels to extract the lead from my blood through a process called chelation.

I spent the next three years in and out of the hospital. Doctors informed my parents that I would be severely disabled because the amount of lead I had ingested was capable of killing five male adults. The disease typically causes brain damage, mental retardation, blindness, and death.

In my unit at the hospital, there were many children poisoned by lead paint. I shared a room with a toddler named Sapphire. We were the same age, and she had severe lead-paint poisoning as well. Nobody ever came to see Sapphire. My mom rocked us both to sleep each night, taking Sapphire under her wing. Mom tells me that we were always holding hands, giving each other strength to get well.

Several months passed and still no family member ever came to visit my surrogate sister. Although they could barely feed their nine children, my mother applied for guardianship of Sapphire. On the day the adoption was to be finalized, and my new sister was well enough to come home, Sapphire's grandmother showed up in court to protest. I never saw Sapphire again.

Back then, the public knew little about the alarming number of children with lead-paint poisoning. In October 1968, my mother became so frustrated by this that she spearheaded a movement to bring about lead-paint poisoning prevention legislation. She began her crusade by asking a group of friends to a meeting in her living room. From there, they formed the Committee for Lead-Based Paint Poisoning Prevention. Mom met with Massachusetts's congressman James A. Burke at the local post office in Canton, Massachusetts, to discuss the drafting of the legislation. Congressman Burke was unrelenting in his effort to draft the initial legislation to protect children against lead paint. He then put it in the hands of congressmen Patrick Moynihan and Daniel Hart in November 1968, and they brought it to Washington.

On December 8, 1968, the muckety-mucks on Capitol Hill invited Grace Agnes Dalton to testify on behalf of the Lead-Based Paint Poisoning Prevention Bill she had championed. In addition to spending her entire emergency fund for the trip (from no less than a dozen coin jars strategically positioned around the house), Mom also borrowed money from a couple of friends to finance her $99 flight. Traveling alone, she left her eight children at home in Boston, while I remained in Children's Hospital for continuing treatment.

My mom was the last to speak in Washington at the Senate subcommittee meeting when Senator Ted Kennedy declared, "We don't have time for you today, Mrs. Dalton. I'm late for a luncheon engagement."

The good senator should have realized you don't butt heads with Gracie Dalton—certainly not when there are TV cameras on the Senate floor.

"Mr. Kennedy," she said in her don't-put-me-off voice, "My baby daughter's in critical condition and you're worried about your lunch?" At that moment, a deluge of cameras surrounded the feisty spitfire whose cheeks flushed as red as her hair. Never mind the *Town Crier*, my mother made the Associated Press and *World News Tonight!* After mom's bold reprimand, the senators graciously deferred.

My mother gave facts about the dangers of lead paint and the number of children dying and being poisoned, and went on to state emphatically, "Lead paint is causing blindness, retardation, and death to as many as one out of every ten children in the city of Boston alone. New York City estimates it has as many as 25,000 cases a year."

She offered solutions such as appropriating federal funds for prevention, detection, and treatment of lead-paint poisoning; de-leading homes; and requiring paint manufacturers to remove lead from paint. She also moved the hardened senators into taking a stand against large corporations poisoning children and against politicians attempting to sweep it under the rug. As the echo of Gracie's last words died away, the silence in the room was electrifying. After a knowing sigh, Senator Ted Kennedy invited Gracie back to his private office where he said, "We need someone like you on our team. Your passion for your cause is commendable. Would you consider coming to work for us in my senate office?"

My mother "Grace-fully" declined. Her goal was to reach as many people as possible about the dangers of lead paint at home in Massachusetts where she began promoting state legislation to combat lead poisoning. For the next five years, my mother went from town to town, speaking and educating about the hazards of lead poisoning.

After the hearing, Senator Edward Kennedy cosponsored and strongly advocated legislation with congressman James Burke, which was filed by congressman William Fitts Ryan.

On January 13, 1971, President Richard Nixon—against the recommendation of his Secretary of Health, Education, and Welfare —signed legislation to combat lead poisoning among children. The bill provided $30 million to be used over eighteen months for prevention, detection, and treatment of lead poisoning.

Grace Dalton received a personal letter from President Nixon on

January 25, 1971, informing her that the legislation was signed into law.

My mother was and is the wind beneath my wings. I can't fathom how she mustered the strength to be by my side *and* fight for the cause, with eight other children at home to care for. I have two healthy children and I have a hard time trying to balance simply working and being home for them. Thankfully, I don't remember much about my long hospital stay as a toddler. When I was young, I sometimes had ugly flashbacks and visions of being strapped to a steel crib with bright lights hurting my eyes. My mother tells me the experimental method used to remove the lead from my system was excruciating. The process can be compared to passing several large kidney stones over many months. Thankfully, I don't remember the pain. I do still have deep scars on my heels from continuously hitting the steel bars on the end of the crib. It must have been my coping mechanism to take my mind off the real pain.

My mother is my hero. To this day, she still advocates for her family and friends. I strive to be half the mother Grace Dalton is. My parents have worked so hard all their lives to raise happy, healthy children. I beam with pride when reminiscing with my siblings about the crusader mom was when we were growing up. She took on our teachers, the state house, bad boyfriends, dishonest neighbors and doctors, to name a few.

One of our favorite stories is about Christmas Eve 1980. My parents and siblings were milling about the kitchen. Dad had just finished preparing a big pot of meatballs, and within minutes they were half gone. The living room was stacked with presents under the tree. Dad was always afraid of fires, so most years we pulled out the fake Charlie Brown tree from the basement. The phone rang and my mother grabbed it off the wall. She had a perplexed look on her face. She tried to quickly uncoil the cord so she could find privacy in the den. Sarah, Patrice, and I crouched by the den doorway to eavesdrop.

Mom blurted out, "Oh no! That's terrible. I'll be right over. No family should be without presents under the tree on Christmas."

My mother grabbed two large, green trash bags and marched into the living room. One by one, she picked up our gifts and put half of them in the bag.

A few of us yelled, "Ma, what are you doing!? Those are our presents!"

"That was Mrs. Patrick. She has nothing to give her five children. She and her husband have been out of work for three months. We have more than enough. I'm giving her half of these gifts."

We were shocked. Those were our presents. Being so young (I was thirteen), we couldn't quite grasp that someone needed those gifts more than we wanted them.

My mother taught us so many lessons. One day, when her time comes to go home to be with her family in heaven, I know she will smile down on us, proudly acknowledging that we have learned and appreciated all her lessons. I am proud to say that I am slowly becoming my mother.

❧

Life sometimes doesn't make sense, especially when we're going through a painful or challenging situation. Even though we may not understand the "whys" of what is happening in the moment, there *is* a reason for everything that occurs. No experience is wasted. Every event is part of a grander plan that ultimately shapes our lives. It's up to us to decide if we are going to be a victim or if we are going to be strengthened by the circumstances. As I reflect on my lead-paint poisoning, I realize that my mom could have sat back, paralyzed by fear and victimization. Instead, she chose to use the experience to make a positive difference for others, and I believe *that* is what we are meant to do with life's challenges.

If you wish to apply this lesson to your life, here's how:

1. Bring to mind a couple of challenging events that you've experienced.
2. Contemplate what possible lessons or spiritual gifts were held within those experiences. A lesson or gift might be a deeper sense of faith, renewed trust, newly discovered strength, an ability to set a boundary or to finally share your truth, a willingness to stand up for yourself or another, the creation of an inspirational product, an opportunity to practice forgiveness of yourself or others, and so on.
3. Now, think about how you might be able to use this lesson or gift to bring peace, joy, or hope into someone's life.

Right now, you don't need to know how you will recognize and pass along your lessons and gifts. Simply trust in the knowing that you would like to use each of your life experiences as stepping-stones to create a purpose-filled life for yourself and others. The "how" will be revealed step by step, inspiring you to make a difference in this world in your own unique way.

There's a chance you might be thinking, *Are you kidding me? I can't see any lesson in this circumstance!* Sometimes, we aren't able to see the gift of the experience because we are still wrapped in the pain of it. If that's your case, here are some peaceful thoughts to contemplate that may help in some small way:

If God leads me to it, I can move through it.
This, too, shall pass.
Pain is inevitable; suffering is optional.
Today, I choose to see that there is Divine Order working in my life.
I let go and let God.

2

Back from the Dead

For almost three years after surviving my coma, I had to return to Children's Hospital regularly for overnight treatments for the lead-paint poisoning. Just before my fifth birthday, I finally returned home for good to our rambling New England farmhouse, comforted by the laughter and shrieks of my eight brothers and sisters. My first night home, as I prepared to drift off to sleep, I watched with wide eyes as a gray-haired, blue-eyed woman wearing a long dress and apron walked about my room as if she were looking for something. Instead of being frozen in fear, I was a bit curious. I looked over at my sisters, Sarah and Patrice, with whom I shared a room, to see if they too saw this woman. They were fast asleep. The woman crept around the room for about five minutes. When she came near me, I felt a chill go through my body and I pulled the covers up to my eyes. I was trying to decide if she was a ghost or a real person. She just seemed to disappear through the bathroom door in my room. Eventually I fell asleep.

The next night, two men appeared in the far corner of my room talking to each other. One was dressed in a black suit and top hat, and the other was in tattered work pants and suspenders. Despite the second man's disheveled look, he smiled warmly and occasionally looked over at me and winked. Again, a chill traveled up by body and I was covered in goose bumps. I could hear them but couldn't understand their words, which sounded like the strange garble you get when you press fast-forward on an audiotape player. Although they didn't seem too interested in me, I felt uneasy. Two nights in a row of unfamiliar people hanging around my room now frightened me a little. Deep down inside I knew they weren't a threat, but I wondered what they wanted. The woman who had come the night before had seemed so familiar and warm, and she didn't talk. But these two men were talking, and they sounded like aliens. I wanted to yell or run downstairs to my mother, but she had strict rules about staying in bed and not making a peep—and I didn't think she'd believe me.

Each night thereafter, I noticed more and more people wandering around my bedroom. By morning the visitors would be gone, and I'd go about my day as any five-year-old would. My two sisters who shared the room were too young to understand what was going on and seemed to sleep through the events. (Sarah was four and Patrice was two). I did ask Sarah if she saw anyone walking around the room at night, and she shouted "No!" and ran away from me.

One night, one of my "visitors" walked into my closet—right through the closed door. Now I knew for sure they were ghosts. They never tried to frighten or hurt me, but sometimes they'd surround my bed and stare. The women looked at me with such compassion and kindness, and would smile and wave. But other times, dogs would appear and surround my bed, barking. *That* scared me! I would lift the covers over my head and pray for them to go away. These visions lasted a couple of months.

Today I understand that my illness and comatose state opened a portal to the other side and these spirits were somehow drawn to me. At the time, though, I couldn't understand why these people were appearing to me. I kept the visions to myself for as long as I could. I didn't think anyone would believe me.

When I finally told my older sisters what'd I'd been seeing, they just chalked it up to side effects of chelation. I approached my sister Maggie, who was ten years old at the time, and said, "There are all these people coming around me in my bedroom at night. I think they are ghosts." I imagine she didn't know what to think of this, but she warned me that if I mentioned the ghosts again, my parents would have to take me back to the hospital. So, I was afraid to tell my parents.

During the day, life was getting back to normal after I came home from the hospital. My younger sisters and I would play with our dolls and, until I was strong enough to go outside, neighborhood friends would come over to play games like Monopoly or Parcheesi. I loved daylight—it meant no ghosts. Most of the time . . .

Being devout Catholics, we had a large picture of the Sacred Heart of Jesus adorning one of the walls in our living room. Every morning, my mom stood in front of this picture saying the rosary, so I knew it was important. In the picture, Jesus stands pointing to his thorn-encircled bleeding heart. His beautiful face has kind eyes that hold the pain of the entire world in their depths. One morning, when I looked over at the picture, I thought I saw Jesus' lips move. I moved closer. The picture was indeed talking to me! In a deep voice, he told me of things to come—things about who was sick or in trouble. He said that my sister, Margaret, had mono, and he also told me that Grammy Mac, my mother's mom who lived with us, would have a heart attack, but that she would be okay. I was too young to understand the magnitude of what was happening (and it would never happen again) or the importance of passing on the information to my mother.

Let me tell you a little about Grammy Mac. Before my mom took over the role, Grammy Mac was head of the God squad in our farmhouse and the glue that held our family together. Towering over me at almost five feet nine inches, with beautiful, piercing hazel eyes, long legs, strong arms, and a hearty laugh, she was a stately woman who took great pleasure in our reactions when she popped out her false teeth and crossed her eyes. She hailed from a family of fifteen in County Donegal, Ireland, where she ran the family farm before immigrating to America. With merely the clothes on her back, she kissed her mother good-bye for the last time and left her family to come to the United States during the depression in Ireland. She met her husband here, settled in Massachusetts, and raised seven children with him. The core of her existence was faith and family. She loved to read scripture—and a good Harlequin romance. Grammy Mac taught my siblings and me to pray the rosary *and* to read tea leaves as we sat around the old woodstove in our living room.

Tea-leaf reading (also called tasseography) is an ancient practice that involves interpreting patterns made by tea leaves left in the cup. Although tasseography is commonly associated with Gypsy fortune-tellers, the tradition of tea-leaf reading arose independently in Asia, the Middle East, and Ancient Greece. Modern tasseography has also been associated with the Scottish, Irish, and cultures in Eastern Europe.

Grammy Mac would brew a pot of Irish tea using only loose tea leaves. She would hand each of us a wide-brimmed teacup. We'd wait until the tea cooled and then drink most of it, leaving a small amount of liquid and the leaves at the bottom. Grammy would tip the cup on its side and carefully drain almost all of the liquid onto a paper towel. We were then instructed to quickly swirl the remaining tea in the cup three times clockwise.

Grammy would put on her thick black-rimmed glasses, which would teeter precariously on the tip of her nose as she peered deep into the cup. She explained that the tea leaves scattered around the cup formed various symbols, numbers, and letters that represented the past, present, and future. Her face would change expression as if she were gazing at an original Picasso. We'd lean toward her, holding our breath and waiting in anticipation for our future to jump out of the cup. Then, without warning, Grammy Mac would look up and shout, "Boo!" We'd jump out of our seats and laugh until we cried. After this game, Grammy would do the actual readings, and quite often, they were incredibly accurate.

Eight days after I'd been forewarned about Grammy Mac's heart attack, my sister Marygrace and I were awakened by sirens in the middle of the night. There was a lot of shouting and stomping downstairs, and we crept to the top of the stairs to see what was going on. My older siblings were huddled downstairs in the hallway watching, and my younger sisters slept through all the commotion. Crouching at the top of the stairs, I saw two men dressed in blue working on Grammy Mac's chest. They put a needle into her arm and hung a bag filled with liquid on a metal pole. I saw them attaching round metal stickers to her chest (that I later learned measured her heart rate). One of the men used his walkie-talkie to speak to someone. I remember some of what he said.

"We have a sixty-five-year-old woman complaining of chest pains. The patient is secure and we're heading to the Goddard Hospital." They quickly wheeled her out of the house on a stretcher. On the front porch, she looked back at us with her signature half-smile as they whisked her away.

Grammy Mac spent the next week in the hospital and then came home—but it wasn't the last she would see of a stretcher. She survived several heart attacks over the next two decades. Each time, she amazed the doctors with her quick recovery and minimal heart damage. Grammy always said, "Leave it in God's hands. When it's my time, it will be my time, and that's that."

We knew she wasn't afraid to die. Grammy couldn't wait to be reunited with her youngest son, Pat, who had been killed in the Korean War at age twenty-two. Twenty years after her first heart attack, their long-awaited "reunion" was at hand. I stood at Grammy Mac's head, gently stroking her hair. Although she had been nonverbal since a stroke the month before, that night she sat up in bed, frantically pointing to the doorway of her room and shouting, "Pat! There's my Pat!" My sister, Elizabeth, grabbed my arm and we just stared at each other in shock. Those of us in the room couldn't see Pat, but we felt his presence. Then, as the room filled with the scent of fresh roses, Grammy Mac passed with her arms outstretched and a huge smile on her face. I was twenty-four years old at the time of her passing.

By the time I reached age nine, I had become an avid reader. But while most of my friends were reading books like *Are You There God? It's Me, Margaret,* I scraped together change from between the couch cushions to purchase Ruth Montgomery books on psychics and past lives. I read *Here and Hereafter, A World Beyond,* and *Born to Heal.* I couldn't get enough of the paranormal. These books explained things I wouldn't dare ask another soul about for fear they would think me weird or different. I'd often lie in bed with a flashlight reading until the wee hours of the morning when the birds started to chirp. My sisters would wake up now and then and yell at me to turn the flashlight off. I hid the books between my mattress and box spring, afraid that my old-school Catholic mother would find them and throw them out.

I learned so much about life after death from these books. My thirst for knowledge on this subject continued into my teen years. I was fascinated with books on many topics, including near-death experiences, life after death, psychic phenomenon, and aliens among us.

In September 1979, when I was twelve years old, my fourteen-year-old sister Marygrace, whom we called MG for short, was walking a lost dog back to its family when she was struck by a car and thrown 500 feet in the air. She landed on the pavement. After being rushed to the trauma unit of Massachusetts General Hospital in Boston, MG was pronounced brain dead. My parents were faced with the agonizing decision to remove her from life support, and the hospital even asked them to donate her organs.

Life support *was* removed, but my mother refused to give up hope. While sitting by MG's bedside, Mom placed her hand in MG's and asked her to squeeze it if MG could hear her.

"Marygrace," Mom said, "if you need to go, then let go. God will take you in his arms. But if it's fighting you want, then it's fighting you've got. We will be right here with you."

At that moment, MG squeezed my mother's hand really hard. The fight had only just begun.

Marygrace remained in a comatose state for almost a year, but my family was with her daily, encouraging her and speaking as if she could hear and understand us. Her eyes wandered around the room, out of focus, but we knew she was in there somewhere. Then, one day, a friend of MG's, with whom she had had a falling out, came to visit.

"Marygrace, Arlene is here," my mother said. "She came to see you."

To our amazement, MG lifted her arm and flipped her estranged friend the bird. We all screamed, and MG smiled. While we never imagined her coming out of the coma like that, it was a joyous moment and we all shrieked in delight, including Arlene. After that, MG started rehabilitation at the Kennedy Memorial hospital, in Brighton, Massachusetts. It was one of the nation's largest pediatric rehabilitation hospitals. MG had a tough, challenging road in front of her. In addition to being completely paralyzed on the left side of her body, she'd suffered brain damage that had her functioning at a five-year-old's skill level, both cognitively and emotionally.

My mother decided to have Marygrace and me confirmed a few months into MG's rehab, right at the rehab center's chapel. (Confirmation is a Catholic sacrament and rite of passage.) Bishop Daniel Hart presided over the ceremony. At this stage in her rehabilitation, MG was not able to stand or walk on her own. She still had a tracheostomy tube in her throat to help her breath but managed to speak through it. Her voice was very raspy. She spent three hours a day in physical therapy trying to learn to walk again, but when her therapists tried to stand her up she would fall down. So at our confirmation, I wheeled MG into the chapel. Then, at the end of the aisle, MG stood up out of her wheelchair. The room let out a collective gasp. Nurses, aids, and family members all rushed to her side. She held us off with her hand and slowly said, "No, I am going to walk to the bishop. Let me walk."

I held my breath as MG slowly and methodically put one foot in front of the other, teetering along the way, finally reaching Bishop Hart. Our family and the staff at Kennedy Memorial Rehab witnessed a miracle that spring day in 1980, and I'm blessed to have been there. In the late 1980s, a popular New England television program called

Chronicle showcased my sister's story and called it "The Miracle Girl."

Because I spent almost every day and night by my sister's side in the rehab hospital in Boston, I missed quite a bit of seventh and eighth grade. My siblings and I went in shifts to the hospital. There would be four or five of us there at one time. When I took a break, I'd often walk around the brain-injury unit looking for young people who had no visitors. My mission was to make them laugh. On the unit I met John, a seventeen-year-old boy in the room next to MG, who had become a quadriplegic after a car accident. I knew that even though he couldn't communicate like everyone else, I sensed I could converse with him telepathically. This was the first time I realized I could communicate in this way. In addition to his being paralyzed from the neck down, the brain injury from the accident left him unable to speak. I could hear him talking to me in my head when I looked in his kind eyes. The first time I walked into his room and introduced myself, I heard in my head the words, *My mother is Linda.*

When the nurse came in, I said, "Is John's mother's name Linda?"

"Yes, it is," the nurse answered. "Do you know her?" Now that I had confirmation that John and I could communicate this way, we would play a game together when others were in the room. I would ask him questions in my mind, and he would smile and blink his eyes in response—slowly for yes and rapidly for no. Sometimes I would hear an actual response in my head from John. I think my little game challenged him and brightened his days and nights. For me, it felt so good inside to share my hidden ability with John and not be judged.

So it was a bittersweet day when Marygrace finally came home from the rehab. I was thrilled she was coming home, but I knew I had to leave my friend John behind. It was late September and the leaves were beginning to change—how appropriate—when I walked into John's room to say good-bye. A single tear trickled down his cheek before I even said a word. I'm not sure if someone told him we were all going home or if it was our telepathic connection. I continued to write him letters for several months until one day a letter was returned marked RETURN TO SENDER, ADDRESSEE UNKNOWN. I sensed that John had finally left the hospital and gone home to be with his family.

During those challenging early teen years, I ached to be normal and tried to bury my special abilities. I stopped talking about the visions and tried to block my telepathic abilities. If my psychic sense picked up something, I ignored it and tried to focus on something else. Eventually, I wasn't "receiving" things like I used to. And I no longer felt weird or different.

In high school I positioned myself as the class clown. This won me friends and, eventually, my big goal: a boyfriend. Because I had planned to become a veterinarian, I attended an agricultural high school. My boyfriend prospects consisted of either Future Farmers of America or "rejects"—city boys sent to the farm for rehabilitation. I ended up with a city boy.

I met Wayne in my sophomore year of high school. He was short, athletic, and very funny. I was bone thin, flat as a board, covered in freckles, and bedecked with braces. I used to run past mirrors without looking at myself, so I really couldn't believe he wanted to date me. I had been convinced I'd go through high school single, but Wayne and

I fit together quite well. Instead of partying with friends, we would sit home, watch the nature channel, and listen to Bob Dylan and Jethro Tull. I played guitar and Wayne played flute. We had grand illusions of starting a band called Nostalgia. We never did, but we did spend the next six years together. I never shared my secret abilities with Wayne, but I often got premonitions about him, gut feelings that I just ignored.

Throughout the last two years of high school, I barely opened a book, but still remained an A student. My test-taking abilities were uncanny; I often chose the correct answer just by tuning in to my intuition. That was a part of my gift I didn't want to squelch.

In my senior year, my best friend Jackie's father suddenly collapsed at home and died. A few days after his services, he appeared to me in a dream. He told me to tell his daughter, my best friend since childhood, that he loved her, that she would always be daddy's girl, and that she shouldn't worry about him.

"Promise me you'll tell her about this," he said.

Although I did promise, when the time came I was too embarrassed to tell her. I was afraid of what she would think of me. Jackie and I eventually lost touch, and I always regretted not telling her. So, several years later, on Christmas Eve, I made a surprise visit to her. After some small talk, I brought up her father and shared some memories I had of him. I finished with, "Do you ever dream about him, Jackie?"

"He comes to me all the time in my dreams. Funny you should ask that," she replied with a curious half-smile.

I took a deep breath and said, "There's something I was supposed to tell you." Jackie waited while I took another deep breath, and then

I said, "Right after he passed, he came to me in a dream. He wanted me to tell you he was okay and you would always be daddy's little girl. He said to tell you how much he loves you. I didn't tell you because I thought you'd think I was a crackpot."

Jackie fell silent, then suddenly began to cry. She thanked me for finally giving her the message and we hugged tightly. It felt good to finally get this off my chest. This was the first time I shared a message from spirit. It had haunted me to hang onto that message and not tell her. I felt so relieved afterward but wondered what Jackie was feeling after I relayed the message.

I'm still not sure if she thinks I'm a crackpot, but I *am* sure that she received the best Christmas present anyone could ever deliver . . . a postcard from heaven.

My early to midtwenties were very difficult years. I began to think I was going a bit crazy. I was petrified of death. Near-death experiences seemed to be commonplace in my family—my lead-paint poisoning coma and my sister's accident, for example—and I developed anxiety and started having panic attacks. I once read that sensitive people sometimes develop anxiety because they don't know how to channel all the energy surging through their system. Plus, I'm an overthinker and a worrywart.

By my early twenties, I had successfully tamped down my abilities to an occasional visit in a dream or random intuitive hits. One of those random hits proved invaluable and possibly saved me from a life of misery. Wayne and I were engaged to be married, and we shared a small one-bedroom apartment. One brisk November day, a "little voice" from my psychic ether told me to go home early from a party at my neighbor's. I often ignored these messages, but this time I didn't and went home earlier than I'd been expected. I walked in to find my fiancé playing naked Twister with Madonna's twin—a woman he'd met at his new job. I was in shock. Even though I had felt the "nudge" to show up, I never imagined the scenario that played out in front of me. My whole world came crashing down.

In hindsight, that pivotal day planted the seeds of a psychic awakening to come that would be beyond my wildest dreams.

Although I was devastated that I had to cancel the wedding and move out of our apartment, I firmly believed that everything happens for a reason. On some level, I think I was relieved that we were breaking up. We were young and didn't have much life experience. Looking back, there are times I want to thank Wayne for following his heart and helping *me* to see a whole new world in front of me. After some time had passed and I'd had a chance to heal, at least partly, I prayed to Grammy Mac to send me my soul mate. (That wasn't too much to ask, right?) And with that, I went looking for him.

Every Friday night, my friend Terry and I would hit the Boston club scene in search of "The One." On a stormy night in March 1992, on my way home from the Roxy, a Boston nightclub, my psychic abilities resurfaced full force—well, more like slapped me in the face. I had just dropped Terry off at her apartment.

"You should really stay over. You look so tired," she said.

"No, I'll be fine. I'm almost home anyway. Don't worry about me."

As I drove away, I ignored that little voice in the back of my head:

You should have stayed. You're running on three hours sleep. You're headed for disaster.

It's okay, I told it. I only have a few blocks to go. I can do this. I'll roll down my windows and sing really loudly.

Ironically, I was rocking out to "I Will Survive" by Donna Summer. And, as it turns out, I would survive, despite the fact I'd unhitched my seat belt because it was digging into my shoulder. My eyes grew heavy as the hypnotic sound of the windshield wipers echoed in my head. I fought to keep them open. *It would feel good to close my eyes right now. Maybe if I just rest them for a second . . .* then the car jumped the curb and hit an old oak tree.

I felt Grammy Mac's presence in the car just before impact and a warm rush of energy surged through my body. I yelled out, but it was Grammy's voice I heard: "Oh, Maureen!" Even as my body hurled forward, I had one split second to wonder why my grandmother's voice was echoing in the car. Then my face hit the steering wheel and bent it in half, and my car was crushed like an accordion.

The next thing I remember is standing outside my car. To this day, I don't know how I got out of the car. My new London Fog raincoat looked like a tie-dyed shirt, with red and orange stripes running down the front. I realized I was bleeding from my face and I needed to get help fast.

Because it was close to two in the morning, the street was dark and empty. I looked over at the house next to the tree I hit. Amazingly, a woman was sitting at her kitchen table reading a book. I knocked softly on the door, not wanting to bother her. I must have looked like a creature from *Night of the Living Dead,* because when she answered the door, she screamed and nearly fainted. She was so hysterical when the ambulance arrived that they put *her* on the stretcher, as I sat nearby, my face buried in a towel. I raised my bloodstained face and weakly called, "Hey."

The fire-rescue team kept asking me who pulled me from the vehicle. (You and I know it was Grammy Mac, but how do you tell that to a paramedic? "Actually, my dead grandmother was in the passenger seat and she pulled me out—after she flew through my body.")

I was rushed to the nearest hospital for immediate triage. Before I was wheeled into the emergency room, a doctor met the EMTs while they were coming through the door.

"Get her up to radiology. She needs a CT scan of the brain right now." If you've ever had a CT scan or MRI, you know the space is very confined and you can't move at all during the procedure. My head and facial injuries were making me nauseous. I was moaning during the procedure and going in and out of consciousness. At one point, I heard a male voice echo throughout the machine. "Maureen, are you alright?"

I was a tad delirious and answered, "God? Is that you? I think I'm okay, but I'm going to be sick."

"Maureen, listen to me. Please look above you."

A shiver went through my body. There was no way I was looking up to meet my maker. Frantic thoughts filled my mind. I did not want to die; I wasn't ready. I had too much to live for. The voice continued, "Maureen, I'm here for you. Please look up."

At this point I was ready to soil myself. I took a deep breath and slowly looked up at the top of the machine. I didn't see God in that moment, but I did see a round speaker in the machine. Giggles emanated through the speaker.

"Maureen, this is Doctor Rabinowitz, the attending physician. I just wanted to make sure you were okay in there."

After the scan was done and the emergency-room doctor finished repairing the gash above my nose, a team of doctors gathered around me.

"Maureen, the CT scan showed several broken facial bones and a fractured skull. We are transferring you to the Massachusetts Eye and Ear Infirmary in Boston. You need specialty care for your facial fractures."

Once I was in Boston, several doctors surrounded the triage bed. They were poking and prodding my eye and nose. I was wheeled away for more tests and told I would most likely need surgery when the swelling went down. My face was now bigger than the Elephant Man's. Many hours later, a tall, thin man with round John Lennon glasses entered the room.

"We've reviewed your scans from the Goddard Hospital, and I just want to go over with you what your condition is. You have a severe orbital fracture on your right eye. All of the tiny bones holding the eye in place are all crushed. We are surprised your eye hasn't sunk back into the socket. Your nose is broken in several places—we're not sure it can be repaired. Above your nasal fracture, your skull is fractured, and there is a hole that needs immediate repair, as spinal fluid is leaking out. We are most concerned about that. You are very susceptible to spinal meningitis. You also have slight fractures on both cheeks and a hairline fracture on your jaw."

As he was telling me this, I felt surprisingly calm. I just knew everything was going to be fine. A few days later, after yet another scan, the eye and nose surgeon came to tell me that I didn't need surgery. He said the cerebrospinal fluid leak in my skull due to the trauma was no longer an issue and they were just going to "keep an eye on things."

"We were going to go in and repair the tear you had in the membrane around your skull. The scan shows that it is healed," said the doctor.

For the next two weeks, doctors and nurses continued to poke around like I was an alien. I knew they were perplexed about my injuries. I had no pain and never once took anything stronger than ibuprofen. Doctors also expected me to have double vision, but I could see fine. My nose looked the same despite being pulverized and I could breathe just fine too.

I've heard traumatic events can sometimes trigger psychic activity. Soon after my miraculous recovery from the accident, I began to sense the spirits again, and I heard hundreds of voices in my head. It was like the mall at Christmas. And there was no snooze button for this reawakening. The deluge of mind chatter drove me crazy at first. I would ask the spirits to talk one at a time. At night, I would beg them to go away so I could sleep. Imagine a theater filled with people talking—that's what it sounded like in my head. I quickly learned that I had no control over the spirits talking to me.

Once I recovered from my accident, I returned to my "normal" life working as a litigation paralegal at a large Boston law firm. While reviewing cases, I started to get nudges from the spirit world pointing me toward pertinent information that could crack the cases wide open and expose fraud. But I couldn't share this with any of my coworkers for fear they would think I was nuts. The attorneys I worked for just thought I was very thorough and had good instincts. Frankly, I continued to be a little freaked out by my newfound ability and by the "friendly voices in the sky," as I called them.

Soon after I returned to work, I met a Native American healer—a shaman—who ran the workers' compensation department in my firm. Had someone sent her to guide me? I believe "someone" did. First, she introduced me to Reiki, the holistic Japanese healing technique that uses gentle touch to balance energy in the body and bring about relaxation and well-being. In addition, she gave me my first books on shamanic healing—*The Way of the Shaman* by Michael Harner and *Spirit Song* by Mary Summer Rain. Both books describe the healing practices and natural wisdom of Native American medicine men and women and promote respect for spirit and the earth. Karen, the shaman at my workplace, who was also a Reiki master, offered to teach me Reiki and help me become certified in all three levels of Reiki healing. The more I learned about alternative healing methods like Reiki and the spirit-based practices of Native Americans, the better able I was to accept and cope with my newfound abilities and the "voices" that accompanied them.

A year after my accident, when I was twenty-five, I met my husband, Greg, at a fifties and sixties club called the Jukebox, which was downstairs from the Roxy nightclub in Boston. Remember how I prayed to my Grammy Mac to send me a soul mate? Well, there was definitely something soulful and familiar about Greg—as if we had known each other before—and we soon fell in love and decided to marry. But how could I begin to warn him that he was about to marry a medium and take the wildest ride of his life? It took time, but Greg eventually came to understand and support my special gifts.

Being newly married brought with it a whole new list of things to stress about—bills, wanting children, saving for a house, getting used to living with someone—and I was already an anxious person. When I was younger I had played the guitar and written music as outlets for my anxiety. Now I needed a new outlet. I decided to try stand-up comedy. Comedy clubs were very popular around Boston then, and Greg and I had our first date at Nick's Comedy Stop in Boston's historical theater district. I was working for the Massachusetts Port Authority at the time and our offices were directly across the street from Nick's. A neon sign at the doorway of the comedy club caught my eye one morning on my way to grab a bagel before work. It read, OPEN MIC NIGHT EVERY WEDNESDAY EVENING—CALL TO REGISTER. I jotted the number down and stuck it in my pocket.

I had always been the class clown, and using my intuition and quick wit was easy for me. Stage comedy turned out to be a breeze. I performed at least once a week at clubs around Boston. I told blonde jokes and made fun of my new husband. Most of my blonde material was written about my childhood best friend Alison. She had moved away to Florida after high school but we still stayed in touch. One summer, Alison called to say she was coming into town and wanted to catch my comedy show. I panicked. She had no idea she was the brunt of my jokes. I had to tell her.

"Alison, there's something I need to tell you. In my act, I make fun of my best friend who is blonde."

Alison paused and said, "Oh my God, does she know? You should really tell her."

"Actually, I'm telling her right now," I said.

"Oh, okay. Do you want me to hold on?"

"Alison, I'm talking about you. You're my blonde friend that I do skits about at my shows."

There was a long, silent pause. *Will she hang up on me?* I wondered. *Maybe she won't speak to me any longer.*

"I am going to be so famous!" she exclaimed.

Greg and I dated for about two years before we got engaged. On a balmy summer evening in 1993, high atop the Prudential skyscraper in the heart of Boston, he got down on one knee and popped the question. The sun was beginning to set behind the infamous CITGO sign behind Fenway Park. In that moment there was nobody else around, or so I thought. My focus was on Greg and his words to me (in between my sobs). When I screamed, "Yes!" the crowd I apparently blocked out erupted in applause. I could feel my cheeks burn as I noticed several people gathered around reaching for a Kleenex.

By noon the next day, several bride magazines covered my kitchen table. As we both came from large families, we understood that our parents could not foot the bill for our wedding. For the next two years, we saved every penny to host our dream June wedding—a simple lakefront reception for 200 guests in Sharon, Massachusetts. It wasn't exactly a *platinum* wedding, but it was worth its weight in gold for us. The wedding party consisted of a mere twenty-six people, mostly made up of immediate family members. The day went off without a hitch— except that the *groom* was late.

Our honeymoon was dreamy—an all-included couples resort in Jamaica. Only this dream quickly turned into a nightmare when we both came down with food poisoning. To top off this romantic occasion, a water main broke in the hotel leaving us with no water for three days. With our "make do" attitudes, we salvaged the end of our honeymoon with a breathtaking trip to the Dunn's River Falls—Jamaica's most famous waterfalls.

Settling into married life was a bit of an adjustment. We both worked long hours in Boston so by the time we got home, Greg was in one room watching sports, while I settled into the bedroom to curl up with a good book or magazine. My desire to learn about natural healing and alternative therapies was at a fever pitch. After becoming certified in Reiki and Native American natural healing, I wanted to add more healing modalities to my repertoire. On the back of a health magazine I was flipping through, there was an advertisement for the Boston Shiatsu School. Shiatsu is an old, traditional Japanese healing method. *Shiatsu* means "finger pressure." The shiatsu practitioner uses palms, fingers, thumbs, knuckles, elbows, knees, and the feet to work on the body's acupuncture points, along what is considered the body's meridians or energy channels. It helps balance an individual's energy flow and strengthen the vital organs.

In shiatsu it is believed that disease is the result of blocked or unbalanced energy, which is either depleted or overactive. Shiatsu shares the same healing viewpoint of harmonizing imbalances in the body's energy as do Chinese acupuncture and Traditional Chinese Medicine.

I cut out the ad and taped it to the mirror on my dresser. Being newly married, money was tight so attending this school right now was just a dream and future aspiration. I was big on manifesting, so I began to tell people in all areas of my life that I was planning on going to shiatsu school one day. I figured it would take at least a couple of years to save for the $4,500 tuition.

In the meantime, I started slowly taking classes locally on stress management, meditation, tai chi, qigong, yoga, herbal remedies, nutrition, and crystals. There was something so familiar about natural healing   I just couldn't get enough. Books on these subjects were scattered all around my bedroom.

Although Greg rolled his eyes every time I brought home a new book, he eventually came around and would ask for help with whatever ailed him at the time.

"My back hurts. Can you do that Reiki thing to me?" He would mumble under his breath.

I would jokingly say, "Okay, let's get this back healed. You're going to need a strong back to carry a little linebacker around."

Talks about having children were usually brought up by me. Greg wanted to wait and do some traveling. Over the next few years we traveled to Florida, California, Canada, and a few Caribbean destinations: Aruba, St. Lucia, the Bahamas, and Mexico.

In·the spring of 1998, my biological clock was ticking so loudly it was waking me up at night. I was thirty-one years old and ready to have a baby. I woke Greg up in the middle of the night.

"Are you sleeping?" I asked.

"What do you think?" Greg replied with attitude.

"Listen, I think it's time we have a baby. I'm not getting any younger, and what if we have trouble getting pregnant?" I announced.

Sighing, Greg sat up and said, "We're not going to have any trouble. Look at my buddy Tom. He and Linda got pregnant on the first try!"

But for Greg and me, as we soon found out, that might never be possible.

<hr />

From the first breath you took at birth to the last breath you take at death, breathing continues to be your constant companion. Use the power of conscious breathing to awaken your intuition and to feel more alive, relaxed, and focused.

"Conscious breathing," by definition, is exactly what it sounds like: It's a natural breathing technique during which you are fully aware of each breath you take. It involves joining each inhalation and exhalation with your conscious awareness and allows your body to release tension and be in the present moment.

The first step in creating calmness and quieting the mind begins with deep breathing from the abdomen. Diaphragmatic or belly breathing helps you to combat stress and to balance and ground yourself. Most people breathe with quick shallow breaths high in the chest when they are tense, anxious, or afraid.

The following exercise will help you develop a calm, receptive, and contemplative awareness.

- Find a quiet place to sit or lie down.
- Turn off your cell phone, television, or any other distractions.
- Take some deep, cleansing belly breaths. Breathe in through your nose, hold it for a count of five, and exhale through your mouth, releasing any body tension.
- Let go of unwanted thoughts and worries. Focus on your breath.
- Imagine that your belly is a balloon inflating on the inhale and deflating on the exhale. Envision a baby sleeping: the belly rises and falls without effort.
- Count your breaths slowly with each inhale and exhale. (This helps keep disrupting thoughts—or "mind chatter"— from slipping in.) If you are limited for time, stop after taking ten breaths. Start with just five minutes a day and work up to at least fifteen minutes.

With practice, the mind chatter will lessen and your body will naturally begin to relax. Optional additions to your "breath break" include gentle music that uses the sounds of the ocean or rainforest; a small trickling fountain placed nearby; sitting or lying outside in nature; and lighting a candle as a focus point.

3

My Miracle Baby

"It is highly unlikely you will be able to conceive. There's a significant incidence of infertility in females poisoned by lead paint. You most likely won't be able to have children," my doctor stated, as if she was informing me that the bathroom was two doors down on the left.

I sat in shock as she shattered my dreams of becoming a mother in that Boston office in May 1998. I couldn't absorb what I had just heard. I didn't *feel* sterile. Not that I knew what being sterile would feel like—but I imagined a stone-cold belly, hollow and numb.

I didn't know how to break the news to my husband, Greg, who'd been secretly buying little football jerseys and newborn Nike cleats. I found them hidden under the bed a few weeks before this appointment.

I had gone in to see the doctor to get a prescription for prenatal vita-
mins. My friend Linda said she started taking them to get her body in
optimal condition to get pregnant.

As I stood outside my apartment building later that day, my body
started to shake and tears welled up. I fumbled through my overstuffed
handbag, desperately trying to find my keys. I just wanted to run up
the stairs and hide under my covers. I was a blubbering idiot before I
even unlocked the door to our one-bedroom apartment. I think Greg
thought someone had died. He came running over to console me.

"I don't think we can have kids. My doctor said I'm 'barren and
cold,'" I cried.

"Come on. Tell me what the doctor *really* said," Greg said.

"Because I had lead-paint poisoning as a child, there's a good chance
I'm infertile. The lead attacks the reproductive organs of females."

"I don't believe her," Greg said. "We should start trying anyway and
see what happens. Mexico is right around the corner. Focus on that and
how much fun we'll have."

We'd booked the Mexico trip to make up for a honeymoon nightmare a few years prior.

I did as Greg suggested, and I began focusing on the trip instead of
on the doctor's dismal news.

When the plane touched down in Cancun the following Saturday,
we jumped on a tour bus to see the Mayan ruins. I had read about
a place called Tulum, which stands on a bluff facing the rising sun
and the Caribbean Sea. The ruins are located on thirty-nine-foot cliffs
along the east coast of the Yucatan Peninsula. Tulum was a major link

in the Mayan's extensive trade network. Both maritime and land routes converged here thousands of years ago.

It was close to a hundred degrees as the sun beat down on my sensitive Irish skin. I could feel my freckles multiplying. Greg wanted to check out the empty graves, so I quickly escaped into one of the ruins' buildings, a place called the "House of Columns." It's a palace-like structure with four rooms whose main entrance faces south. Six columns support the roof of the main room, and there's a roofed sanctuary. I had to duck my head to enter the stone structure. There were three archwayed corridors to choose from once inside—I went to the right.

The heat was taking its toll, and I just had to sit down. I found a short cement pole to rest my nearly sunstroked body on. As I sat down, a cool chill ran up my spine. I recognized this feeling. When I had seen spirits as a child, I felt a chill first, and I now recognized it as energy. But here this wasn't just any energy—this was *power plant* energy. I felt like there were a hundred eyes on me in that semidark, cavelike space. Then I heard giggles behind me. I quickly glanced over my shoulder but nobody was there—nobody I could see.

"You're sitting on the Mayan fertility pole," a Mayan tour guide said, appearing as if out of nowhere.

"Oh," I said with a laugh. "That's pretty funny. I don't really have to worry about that."

"No worries," he said as he began to turn away.

I dropped my head for just a second and when I looked up, he was gone. Less than a moment later, Greg appeared in the entranceway. "There you are!" he said with relief.

I quickly told him about the exchange with the Mayan guide. "You must have just passed him on your way in," I said.

"Nope, I didn't pass anyone. It's just you and me. You must *really* have heat stroke. Let's get you to the hotel," Greg said with a reassuring smile.

Once inside the hotel room, I collapsed onto one of the double beds and Greg plopped himself onto the other. He was out cold and snoring in less than two minutes. As I started to drift off to sleep, three Mayan men approached the bed and surrounded me. I vaguely recall thinking I might be dreaming. The men wore colorful sashes with bright orange, maroon, and yellow stripes over a white shirt and loose-fitting red pants. One of them leaned over the bed and whispered in my ear. I was frightened and tried to move but found that I couldn't. I hadn't quite heard him, and I managed to ask him to repeat what he said. Then I heard loud and clear, "Your mother has had a heart attack. She is in a hospital in Ireland. You must call home." Then they left my bedside and walked *through* the door. I couldn't believe what had just happened. I understood now that they were spirits, and I felt privileged to have received this information and blessed that they knew I would listen and eventually understand.

Several years earlier, my mom had had her first heart attack at age fifty. We'd been sitting in the den when she started rubbing her shoulder. Immediately, I heard *a voice* in my head: *she's having a heart attack.*

I stood up. "Mom, I think you're having a heart attack. Let's go to the hospital."

"No, I'm fine," She replied. "I think I just hurt my shoulder . . . but, the pain *is* going into my back and now my jaw hurts."

Though I was afraid she wouldn't believe me, I told her about the little voice in my head: "Mom, I keep hearing someone tell me that you're having a heart attack. They are telling me you need to go to the hospital now. I don't know who it is, but they said you could die."

She just stared at me for a moment, then said, "Okay, let's go."

In the waiting room at the local ER, my sister Rose and I tried to keep Mom calm by talking about lighthearted things. When the nurse came over to us, my mother started joking with her, but then suddenly grabbed her chest and began gasping for breath. This was clearly a massive coronary. The waiting room quickly filled with hospital staff, and we were asked to leave the room. Once Mom was stabilized, she was transferred to the New England Deaconess Hospital in Boston for triple-bypass surgery.

Now, several years later, when the Mayan spirits told me my mother was having another heart attack, I knew it could very likely be true. Despite my previous exhaustion, I jumped out of bed and called my parents' home in Stoughton. I knew they were in Ireland, but I had a feeling one of my siblings would be there and have news for me. My sister Elizabeth answered the phone.

"Is Mom in the hospital? Did she have a heart attack?" I blurted out.

"Oh my God, I just hung up the phone with Dad . . . Mom *is* in the hospital in Dublin with chest pains. How the hell did you know that?" she asked.

"Some ancient Mayan men came into my hotel room and told me Mom had a heart attack."

"Huh? How did they get a key to your room?" Liz asked.

"Lizzy, there were spirits, ghosts . . . you know, the *see-through* kind."

Although Lizzy knew I had visions and spooky encounters on occasion, she didn't like to talk about anything paranormal. (In fact, she often slept with a light on to keep away [her words] the Boogie Man.)

"I gotta go," she said now. "That stuff creeps me out. I'll call you later with an update on Mom."

When I returned home a few days later, my mom called me from Dublin and told me that the doctors believed she'd had a mild heart attack. I was grateful the Mayans had given me this information because my siblings would have waited until I got home to tell me.

About a month after the Mexico trip, I started having sharp pains in my lower belly. Thinking it was an ulcer from worrying about my mother's health, I went to see my doctor. After a brief discussion and some minor tests, she decided to check for an ovarian cyst. When she did the exam, a perplexed look came over her face. When I sat up, she handed me a urine stick.

"I'm pretty certain you're pregnant," she said. "Use this and come right back."

My thoughts immediately turned to the fertility pole I'd inadvertently sat on in the Mayan ruin in Tulum. *Had the Mayans sent me a blessing? Could I really be pregnant?*

Much to my and my doctor's surprise, I *was* pregnant! I *had* received a miracle in Mexico. When I told Greg, he was both shocked and ecstatic. The second thing out of his mouth after "Wow!" was "What will you do about shiatsu school?"

I had already enrolled in the Boston Shiatsu School in Cambridge, Massachusetts, and was to start in a few weeks. It took three years to save enough for the down payment to help make this goal of mine a reality. Shiatsu is generally performed on a futon mat on the floor. Greg was worried it would be too much for me with my new pregnant status. After careful thought, I decided to continue to pursue my dream to learn shiatsu.

I couldn't wait to tell my family about the baby. I know that most couples wait until the scary first trimester ends before they spread the joyous news, but I was busting at the seams. I told my mom first. I informed her that I was two weeks, three days, and ninety-seven minutes pregnant. As with most breaking news given to Gracie, she responded with, "I know. I've been praying hard to Grammy Mac."

By the end of the first trimester, I could feel little "pops" in my belly. Although the doctor said I wouldn't feel kicking until fifteen or sixteen weeks, I was so in tune with my body that I knew it was my miracle baby reminding me he was there. My sister Liz, who's the unofficial "doctor" of our family, tried in vain to convince me the "pops" were just gas.

I continued my grueling schedule of working at Logan Airport, going to shiatsu school, and doing stand-up occasionally at a Boston comedy club. Being pregnant provided a lot more material. My husband, Greg, accompanied me to every comedy show. If anyone heckled me, Greg would zing them with a comeback that would make any human blush.

My schedule was very full to say the least. I would leave my apartment at 7:00 AM, travel to work at Logan Airport (taking a train, a boat, and walking along Boston harbor). I left Logan at 5:00 PM to travel to Cambridge three nights a week, by boat, bus, and subway for the start of shiatsu class at 6:00 PM. Class went until 10:00 PM. I then walked down Mass Avenue in Cambridge to the Porter Square T stop (underground subway), which took me to South Station in Boston to pick up the commuter rail to my apartment in Stoughton. I arrived home close to midnight. When I didn't have class, I left Logan and traveled over to Nick's Comedy Stop in the theater district or the Comedy Connection in Boston's famous Faneuil Hall to let off some steam on stage.

Toward the end of my pregnancy with my miracle baby, I had another scare, a huge one. During a routine ultrasound, the technician had a perplexed look on her face as she moved closer to the monitor. I could feel in my gut that something wasn't right.

"I'm going to go get the doctor," she said, faking a smile.

The doctor, a petite woman with short blonde hair, rushed into the room and grabbed the ultrasound wand to run over my lubed belly. She held nothing back. "I've never seen anything like this. Your fetus has two large tumorlike growths on its eyes. If you don't mind, I'm going to call the team of surgeons in. In all my years of practice, I've never seen this before. I'll be right back." I was shocked at her cold delivery of such disheartening information. I felt like the wand was a stun gun, and she had just double-zapped me. *My precious miracle baby will be blind? Oh my God, maybe it's cancer!* My mind was racing with thoughts of the worst-case scenarios.

Eight doctors—five women and three men—quickly pushed open the door to the ultrasound room. They surrounded the monitor. Only two actually looked at me. The blonde doctor took the stun gun and pushed it so far into my belly I thought I would pop. A collective "ahhhh" filled the room.

She spoke to her colleagues as if I were merely a fly on the wall. "After delivery, we'll have to take the baby and operate immediately. We'll consult with Massachusetts Eye and Ear (one of the finest specialty hospitals in the world). There is a chance this baby will be blind and have no tear ducts." I could say nothing. I was in such shock I was numb. I wanted to scream, "No! Not my perfect baby? Why?"

Oh, no, you don't! I thought to myself. *I'm going to call on all my angels, guides, dearly departed loved ones, Mary the blessed mother of God, God, Jesus, Buddha, Zeus, Mother Theresa, and anyone else in spirit I can think of. Whatever healing my child needs, let it be. My prayers will be answered.*

I held my hands on my belly every chance I had. Warmth flowed through me to my baby as I visualized the tumors melting away like icicles on a fifty-degree winter's day. I prayed the Catholic prayers I had learned as a child—the Hail Mary and Our Father—and also said Native American prayers I had learned from a Lakota shaman.

Talking to my precious baby while I cradled my belly with my hands helped immensely. I felt like we were bonding and he recognized my voice. He squirmed and hiccupped during my hands-on sessions. (We found out he was a boy on Christmas Eve. I had asked the ultrasound tech to write the gender on a card and seal it in an envelope, which I placed under the tree. When I opened it, out popped an ultrasound picture with a circle around the nether regions and an arrow marked with the word "penis" pointing to it.)

When I went back to the hospital a month later for a follow-up ultrasound, the doctor was eagerly waiting with a team of surgeons and students. She grabbed her trusty ultrasound wand like it was a sword and she was Xena, the Warrior Princess, and dug in, thrusting the wand deeper and deeper, trying desperately to find images of the tumors. But they were gone. Completely gone.

"I don't know what to tell you," she said, "but the eye growths have dissipated and are untraceable."

I thought about mentioning my prayers to Jesus, Buddha, and Mother Theresa, but I didn't want to pop her medical bubble. The team walked out of the room like they had just lost the World Series. Because I was in a teaching hospital, a unique opportunity for them to observe and learn had just flown out the window. I'm sure they were relieved for me, and just a little bit disappointed.

Two weeks later, I sat at my desk at Logan International Airport gazing at planes taking off from my office window. It had always amazed me that they didn't turn too far and crash right into my building. In fact, they were often so close I had a ritual of jumping up to wave to some of my favorite pilots from Federal Express and Cape Air.

In May 1999, I went into labor in my office. It was time for me to fly . . . to the hospital. I called Greg, who worked at State Street Bank in downtown Boston. He rushed over to pick me up and we headed to Brigham and Women's Hospital. It wasn't a good idea to go into labor at 3:00 PM during rush hour in Boston. We were completely stopped in traffic on Storrow Drive as my contractions got stronger and closer together.

I jumped out of the car, pacing and yelling, "I'm in labor. Move out of the way. Help!"

You have to understand the people of Boston. They are not shocked or moved by much. Most people just rolled up their windows and turned away. I'm not sure what I expected—maybe a doctor "in the house," or the cars to hit their hidden jets and turn sideways to make room for the only pregnant woman in Boston.

I finally arrived at the hospital. When they put the monitor on my belly to see how far apart the contractions were, they told me the baby was in distress. The nurse pointed out that the monitor report showed a delay in the baby's heartbeat every time I had a contraction. She was convinced the umbilical cord was wrapped around his head. They whisked me away to labor and delivery. The doctor reached inside me and inserted an internal fetal monitor. The fetal monitor measures the heartbeat in a more precise way than the external monitor. Then, everything stalled. I went from 3 centimeters to 3.1 centimeters in twelve hours.

Next, they gave me Pitocin. This drug is the brand name of a synthetic form of oxytocin, a contraction-causing hormone made in a woman's brain. Pitocin can initiate or augment labor by making contractions stronger and more frequent. The bottom line is Pitocin makes you feel like your insides are turning inside out. I was given a double dose of Pitocin when things were not progressing like the doctors thought they should be. Remember that commercial, "This is your brain on drugs," with a picture of an egg frying in a hot pan? My brain felt like it was sizzling, much like a frying egg. I started doing tai chi (a gentle Chinese martial art practice) and qigong exercises (a moving meditation to cultivate energy in the body) to ease the pain and anxiety.

For the next couple of hours, I continued doing tai chi and qigong until the doctor finally said I was fully dilated and ready to get back in bed to start pushing. Four hours into pushing, the baby's heartbeat stopped. My blood pressure plummeted to 60/22. I looked at Mary, my labor and delivery nurse, and asked her, "Are we dying?"

The look on her face answered my question. The doors to the delivery room flew open and four people dressed in white coats came running over to me. They banged on my belly and yelled, "Emergency C-section!" I heard a voice in my head say, *Flip on your right side.* So, I yelled out, "Flip me on my right side, now!" Mary and my doctor lifted me up and slammed me down on my right side. I could hear a faint, "blip, blip, blip" as the monitor picked up a weak heartbeat from the baby.

I began pushing again and could finally see his furry little head. His hair was strawberry-blond, like mine. Then his heartbeat stopped again. He was stuck in the birth canal. The doctor who was filling in for my regular obstetrician seemed panicked. She said she could use the vacuum or forceps.

I yelled, "Get the vacuum *now!*"

The vacuum is a plastic cup that is placed on the baby's head and attached to a suction device. I must have had the king of all Hoovers because when the vacuum pulled my baby out, I was ripped and torn from what felt like my head to my big toe. But at that point I didn't care if they cut my entire body open. I just wanted my boy to be okay.

Two days, twelve hours, and thirty-two minutes after arriving at the hospital, Tyler James Hancock entered this world and took a look around the room as a nurse placed him in the incubator and took him to the neonatal intensive care unit for observation.

It took almost four hours to stitch the level-4 tear in my nether regions (no other levels after that one!). About two hours into the repair, the fill-in doctor (who looked like a twelve-year-old Dakota Fanning) looked at me and said, "Ummm . . . I did it wrong. I have to take all these stitches out and get some assistance."

Whadda ya mean, you did it wrong?! I thought. *What does that mean?! Is my path crooked? Did you sew the whole thing shut?*

She left the room and came back with the hospital's chief of surgery. He was a tall, slim man who didn't crack a smile. I was so tired I started to get a little punchy. As he began the descent to repair the levy, I had an idea. *Tap, tap, tap.* (I tapped him on the shoulder). "Knock knock," I said. I was determined to make him smile. No response. "Knock knock, I said!"

Unimpressed, he made a feeble attempt to play my game. "Who's there?"

"Annoying starfish."

He continued to stitch away as if he had a deadline to finish a needle-point piece for the state fair. "Annoying starfish who?" he responded.

I laid all five fingers on his face, perfectly separated like a spider. To my surprise, he actually chuckled.

"Miss, you are going to have some problems down here if you don't let me finish."

He had a point.

When I finally held my little miracle boy almost six hours later, he looked up at me like he'd known me for a thousand years. I melted when he wrapped his tiny fingers around my index finger. Little did we know, however, that there would be one more challenge to conquer. In labor, Tyler and I had spiked high fevers. They wanted to give me antibiotics as a precaution.

"I've been allergic to all the antibiotics I've ever taken," I said fearfully.

The doctor said, "Well, we'll try something you haven't taken before, gentomycin and clydomycin."

Once again, my instincts started kicking in, and taking antibiotics just didn't feel right. I knew I should have stopped the process. Have you ever just known something was going to go wrong and didn't or couldn't find your voice to stop it? Everything at that moment told me to stop them from starting the IV. I just figured they knew what they were doing, so I didn't say anything. The nurse loaded the bag on the IV stand, and I watched the liquid drip into my arm.

About a half hour later, as I lay watching *Saturday Night Live* with Greg, my feet started to tingle. As Chris Farley's words, "In a van down by the river" echoed in my head, I couldn't feel my legs. It felt like someone had draped my legs with a heavy X-ray apron.

"I can't feel my legs," I said, my voice panicked. "Hit that nurse button on the wall and call for help," I cried frantically.

Greg is the type of guy who has a fight-or-flight response in times of panic, and he usually takes flight. For instance, once when I asked him to call 911 because Tyler was turning blue from whooping cough in the middle of the night, he yelled, "I don't know the number!"

Now, he couldn't locate the red, tennis ball–sized button with a nurse icon on it.

The numb feeling quickly traveled up my arms and through my torso. The next words out of my mouth sounded something like this, "Hiiith tha thutton, health me, um thying."

I felt myself fading fast, going into anaphylactic shock. Greg finally found the panic button and hit it.

"How can we help you?" a nurse said in a tired voice.

"I canth bweath!" I yelped with all the strength I had left. My tongue began to swell, and I started to gag.

"Code blue, code blue, room 1021!" the intercom rang out. Lights flashed and a siren sounded as if we'd just escaped from Alcatraz. The code team came dashing into my room. I was surrounded by people in white (here and "there"). I could see my grandmother in spirit behind me on my left side. She had her hand on my shoulder. There was no expression on her face. There was a man in spirit with long, wavy blond hair and stunning blue eyes, standing in the corner of the room smiling. He looked like Fabio. I wondered if he could have been a spirit guide or guardian angel.

I felt like I was sinking into the bed. The nurse taking my blood pressure looked panicked. I felt a sharp jab in my thigh. They administered epinephrine (adrenaline). Epinephrine prevents worsening of the airway constriction and has a suppressive effect on the immune system. I felt like I was leaving my body . . . possibly for good. The room kept getting smaller and smaller, and it seemed as if I were floating near the ceiling, watching these people work on me. I remember thinking I would never get to see my baby again. I could see Grammy Mac waving to me in the distance. I thought I was dreaming. Everything felt calm and euphoric. I wanted to stay in that feeling, as if I were wrapped in a warm cocoon.

I felt a powerful push and suddenly, I could feel my arms and legs again! I was back in my body. Most importantly, I could breathe. I gave thanks to the Mayans for the fertility pole that brought me here (okay, thank you, too, Greg), all the angels and saints, God, Buddha . . . well, you get the picture. I think I even thanked the janitor who came to clean the bathroom (in my delusional state, I believe I tried to have him check on my nether region for swelling after those 200 stitches). He spoke broken English, "No, no, not doctor, mop mop."

The funny thing about people is that sometimes they can be wrong, and that includes doctors. Their job is to guide us the best way they know how with the tools they have been trained with, but life isn't always set in stone. Sometimes, a miracle awaits, and we just need to be able to see the path to it.

Think of how a navigation system works in your car. It is connected to a satellite that always knows where you are (except on super cloudy days). You punch in the desired direction you want and—voila!—the GPS begins giving you guidance step by step. Now, I don't know about you, but when I first started using my GPS, I argued with it! When I would stubbornly take a different route, not wanting to trust her (mine is set to a sassy English chick I call Ella), she always gently and lovingly repeated, "Recalculating." She's always right, and I've learned to trust her (mostly).

Inside each one of us is a built-in guidance system, an inner knowing that is connected to divine guidance. It's been there since birth and will always let us know when we're "off course." Are you paying attention to it? Here are some ideas to help you tune in to your very own GPS:

1. Know where you want to go. What dream is within your heart? Plug that into your inner navigation system. (In my case, I wanted to have a healthy baby!) Share it with God, your angels, your loved ones in spirit, anyone you envision as a higher power.

2. To thine own self be true! Have faith and trust, and know that anything is possible, even if you can't see how. If well-meaning friends or family members tell you that you can't or won't achieve your heart's desire, they are simply saying that from their frame of reference, which may have nothing to do with your life. I'm sure they mean well, but they may not have a miracle mind-set. I do believe that anything is possible for those who believe! Who in your life can be your champion and help you stay tuned to a miracle mind-set in moments of doubt or uncertainty?

3. Let go of how you think something is supposed to come into your life, and be prepared for anything. But follow up

on the little hits of divine guidance that come into your
mind, even (and especially) if you don't know why. Those
hunches are like Ella, my GPS, telling me,
"Right turn in 100 yards."

Now, a word about these little hunches: they can come
to you as a thought, or in a dream, or you may hear or feel
them. Pay attention . . . they are there. How do you receive
those hunches, those little "hits from heaven?" What are
they nudging you to do?

4. Remember, this is your dream, and you are so worthy and
   deserving of it. Act as if everything is possible. Move
   in the direction of your dream. What is one step you can
   take today to realize your dream? Do it . . . you'll be glad
   you did!

4

Postcards from Heaven

We took Tyler home to our small but cozy one-bedroom, third-floor apartment in Stoughton, Massachusetts, which was just down the street from my childhood home. Although I wasn't quite finished with shiatsu training, my mother—who served on the board of directors for the local hospice—couldn't wait to spread the word about my healing work. I didn't feel prepared to start taking clients, but when cancer patients began calling and asking for my help, I decided to see them. I explained to both my mother and my clients that I could not heal them, but I could empower them to heal themselves. I was already certified in Reiki and in Native American studies, and, because of previous classes I took to help relieve my own stress and anxiety, as well as the countless books I've read on the subject, I started to teach stress management to various companies.

Old friends, neighbors, and mostly strangers I had never met before flocked to see me. People who could barely walk climbed three flights of stairs to lie on a futon mat in my living room.

Little miracles occurred along the way. Some clients reported their tumors had disappeared or shrunk, while others reported relief from pain. I knew I was being used as a conduit for great things. Not everyone was completely healed, but most clients received some form of relief. Healing sessions for those with cancer were (and still are) offered at no cost. For all other clients, a sliding payment scale was in place to ensure nobody was turned away for lack of funds.

One day during my early years practicing, my friend Laura called me in a panic.

"Maureen, Brian is on the floor crying in pain. He can't move. Tomorrow, he's scheduled for back surgery. They want to fuse his spine. Is there any way you can come over and help him?"

I grabbed my coat and scooted out the door. Laura greeted me at the door with tears in her eyes. She pointed to the kitchen and I walked in. Her husband, Brian, was lying in the fetal position whimpering. I sat on the floor next to him and put my hand on his lower back. In my mind, I had no idea how to even begin to help this man. I prayed to the Blessed Mother Mary to assist me in this session. I gently began to palpate pressure points on Brian's back, next to his spine. As I held my hands over his lower back, I could feel heat flowing through my hands.

"Wow, your hands are like heating pads. I can already feel the pain lifting. What are you doing?" Brian asked.

"Ah, well, a hodgepodge of everything. I'm using Reiki energy, acupressure, and prayer."

After about a half hour, Brian slowly got up from the floor. He started crawling around the kitchen.

"I think I can stand up. I can't believe what you did. I'm not feeling any pain at all."

He grabbed my arm and started to stand up slowly. This may come as quite a shock, but he literally started to do an Irish jig.

"Look, I can dance!" he said smiling.

I couldn't believe my eyes. Laura stood in the doorway stunned. Her mouth was wide open and tears streamed down her face.

The next day, she called to tell me that Brian was doing great. He put off the surgery for the spinal fusion and has been fine ever since.

When Tyler turned six months old, we bought our first home—a small two-bedroom white cape in Bridgewater, Massachusetts, where we still live today. I left my job at Logan Airport to practice shiatsu out of my new home and to allow me to make home visits to people who were too ill to travel to me. Tyler would go to his grandmother's house on days I would see clients.

After I began treating people regularly, I started to notice a strange occurrence as I massaged people's feet. Without fail, a spirit message would come through with every foot massage. I think the clients' deep relaxation allowed the spirits to communicate a message or two. In the beginning, the messages were quite similar: "Tell them I'm okay. I don't feel like I've left them, and I'm not missing out on their lives."

For example, once, at the end of a long day, I was kneading a client's aching feet during a particularly concentrated shiatsu treatment at my home. She looked so relaxed compared to how agitated she'd been when she arrived. Her body seemed to melt into the floor as the treatment went on. Suddenly, as I touched the sole of her foot, a crowd of spirits came marching in one by one. They were all talking over one another. The chatter slowed down, and I heard a woman's voice muttering something. I couldn't quite make out what she was saying. It was like trying to tune into an AM radio station. Then all the voices finally quieted down as the special guest spoke louder. "I'm her mother, Angelina," the voice informed me. "Tell her I'm here. I'm Angelina."

As much as I didn't want to interrupt the massage or disturb my client's deep relaxation, her mother's voice was insistent. I could not hold back this communication and gently whispered, "Your mother's name is Angelina, isn't it? And she's from New Jersey, right?"

Buzzkill. My client's arches cramped, her eyes widened, and she peeked up at me over her shoulder and said, "My mother passed away three years ago. How do you know her name?"

"I heard it in my head. As I was massaging your feet, I kept hearing loud voices echoing in my head. Then I heard a woman say she was your mother, Angelina. She kept asking me to tell you she was here. She also said she was the obnoxious Italian from New Jersey." My client was speechless.

"Your mother just wants you to know she is still with you. She was very insistent I let you know she is here," I told her.

She got up off the futon mat and gave me a big hug.

"I feel like I'm hugging my mother one more time. Thank you."

This same scenario played out frequently with my clients. I tried to explain to them what was happening and did my best to assure them I wasn't crazy or hadn't been picking through their trash to learn things about them. Soon enough, it became commonplace for my massage therapy clients to leave teary-eyed and wanting more . . . *messages,* not *massages.*

My husband became suspicious of these tearful guests and finally broke down and asked what I was doing to my clients. Greg is a "manly man," and what I like to call a healthy skeptic. Early in our relationship, he often playfully dismissed my comments about knowing things and communicating with the dead. When I began practicing in earnest, I explained to Greg what was happening during my massage appointments, but also that I didn't know quite *how* it was happening. In the beginning he just rolled his eyes. Soon, however, this believer in Red Sox dreams would jump on my spirit bandwagon and accept that I really did have a gift. I think what finally convinced him were the clients who would stop to say good-bye to him and make comments like, "Hey, your wife is pretty amazing. She just told me my dad's name and how he passed, and said things only he would know."

Word quickly spread that a woman on Sunset Drive could heal anything from migraine headaches to food allergies. But let's be clear here, I never claim, or claimed, to be a healer. I am simply a conduit that helps people connect to their own inner healing ability. Their path to healing simply needs a jump start, and I just happen to be holding the jumper cables.

Within a few short months of starting to see clients in my new home, I couldn't keep up with the requests for "that thing you do with your hands." I knew it was time to take my clients out of my house and into a real office space. My sister Rosie, who owned a flower shop in the next town over, quickly offered me her storefront as well as her assistance.

"Yeah, I'll clean out a room in the back and do my massage out of there," I said.

"No, I mean you can use my entire storefront," she explained. "I don't want to do flowers anymore."

"When do you think you'll shut down the flower business?" I asked.

"Tomorrow," she said without hesitation.

We both burst into laughter. I've always admired Rosie's do-it-now attitude. One of her favorite sayings—and I live by this too—is, "If it's not an absolute yes, then it's a no."

Rosie closed her shop the next day, and I opened my practice, Pathways to Healing, the following week. Again, word spread like wildfire throughout our close-knit community, and we were receiving twenty to thirty calls a week without advertising.

Through local hospices, the news spread that I provided free holistic healing and massage to cancer patients. I traveled to hospitals, homes, and hospices. The *Middleboro Gazette*, a local paper, got wind of my charitable work and published an interview with me in the fall of 2001.

I knew I needed to put a name to my vision. I researched how to start a nonprofit organization and named it Manifest a Miracle. The name reflected my belief that each person has the ability to manifest something miraculous—whether it is pain relief, a new, positive attitude, or even a cure. (Today, Manifest a Miracle is called Seeds of Hope. Several years ago, my dear friend Sandy Alemian and I began working together and merged our two foundations. She had formed the first "Seeds of Hope" after her infant daughter passed away.)

I've always felt a calling to assist the sick and dying. It's not like anyone close to me ever suffered with cancer, it's just something I've said since I turned five. Maybe it was due to my experience at Children's Hospital when I was young—seeing all those sick children suffering with illness and cancer. My teachers would ask, "What do you want to be when you grow up, Maureen?"

My answer never changed: "I want to help sick people. I want to make them feel better.

I tried to personally handle all the requests that came in after the newspaper article ran. At one time I was seeing fifteen clients a week in Massachusetts and Rhode Island. My heart was exponentially bigger than my bank account and soon the "blue" bills piled up. You know, the ones that say, "FINAL NOTICE." Still, I always tried to keep things in perspective, and my sobering thoughts were always the same: *At least I have my health. I don't have cancer.*

I finally broke down and reached out for assistance. I knew I needed to bring in other practitioners to take on some of my clients. I couldn't expect everyone to volunteer their time, so I knew I had to hold a fundraiser, and fast, to support my vision.

Greg was shocked when I told him a week later that I had booked a

fund-raiser for my newly formed cancer foundation. I was calling the
fund-raiser "Postcards from Heaven." His shock wasn't so much at the
name of the event, but at the *host* of the event—me!

I envisioned a room full of people who'd lost loved ones. I'd tell my
story and then walk around the room relaying messages from these
loved ones in spirit. My previous experience with public speaking and
stand-up comedy gave me the confidence I needed to stave off any
stage fright. I had also taught stress management to large corporations,
medical facilities, and public-sector employees, combining humor
with my holistic healing training, so I really was comfortable with large
groups of people.

My friend Dina donated a function room at her popular restaurant,
the Fireside Grille, in Middleboro, Massachusetts. We decided to offer
a stuffed-chicken dinner, much like a wedding function. Only this
time the guest list would include the living *and* the dearly departed.

With mostly word of mouth and local support, the event took off
and sold out within a few weeks. I was stunned. I felt humbled by the
number of people reaching out in hopes of having a hello from heaven
or that last good-bye.

My friends all pitched in. They collected tickets at the door, ushered,
and announced me. The line of people waiting to get in stretched down
the hall and out the door, almost out of the parking lot. Before I was
introduced, I peeked around the corner to see the end of the line, and
my heart pounded against my chest. My hands instantly got clammy
and I felt the heat in my cheeks. I took a deep breath and paced back
and forth behind the stage. *So, this is what stage fright felt like.* It was

quite unexpected. So much for "Miss Nerves of Steel."

The audience included small children and senior citizens, but mostly women in their thirties to fifties. Everyone seemed excited and curious, even the half dozen men who showed up at the event with their eager partners. The elderly women held tight to their grandchildren, perhaps hoping their fears of death would be lifted or a husband would come through to ease their grief.

At least a dozen people waited in line at the bar. I attributed this to nerves. I've since learned that most mediums don't allow alcohol at demonstrations. As long as the drinking isn't in excess, I am fine with it. Alcohol can lower the vibration of energy and make it harder to connect.

As I looked out on the long, oval-shaped room, my thought process went something like this: *Oh my God, what was I thinking?! There must be two hundred people out there, and they are expecting me to connect with their dead relatives! I'll have to ask them to take off their shoes so I can rub their feet first . . . I can't do this. I'll just tell them nobody showed up from the other side. They must all be busy with other things. Enjoy the chicken.*

Being a good Irish Catholic girl, I said a quick Hail Mary and ran on stage . . . well, actually, I believe someone from the other side pushed me. My natural gift of humor came pouring out and as each second passed, I became more comfortable introducing the show by sharing my story. I could feel the tension in the air as all eyes were on me—some people expecting miraculous messages, others fearing that I would start to channel the spirits like Whoopi Goldberg in the movie *Ghost*: "Orlando, is that you? Damn baby, what'd you do to your hair?"

After my impromptu beginning, I felt ready to welcome the "special guests" in. *I* was ready. The *spirits* were not. There was nothing but a blank screen in my mind—nothing, nada, zippo. My face grew hot, and I scanned the room for the EXIT sign. All eyes were on me as I walked around the room. Finally, with nothing to report, I came to a stop and leaned on one of the audience member's chairs for support.

Suddenly, I heard a loud booming sound. In my mind's eye, I saw the explosion connected to the sound and a man being thrown. I also heard the name "Rose."

"Did someone lose their husband in an explosion? Rose?" I blurted out.

Silence. You could have heard a feather drop.

Then, the woman whose chair I had leaned on, a blonde woman in her forties, dropped her head in her hands and began to weep.

The woman in the chair beside her, apparently her friend, called out, "Her name is Rose and her husband died in an explosion!"

It took me a moment to catch my breath, both physically *and* mentally, as it always does when the spirits come. The excitement and shock I feel when a spirit's messages are confirmed by a loved one never gets old. This particular man's spirit felt so strong and I knew he wanted to connect with his wife very badly. For a moment, I wished everyone else would leave so I could spend the next three hours comforting Rose. She slowly stood up. She was petite, with beautiful soft brown eyes. I took her hand and looked deeply into those eyes.

"He is fine. He says he wasn't supposed to be in the building. I hear the name Bill."

She took the microphone and said, "His name is Bill. He went into work on his day off and the building exploded."

As I heard Bill's message, I went on to talk about his three children and the upcoming wedding of their son. "He will be there at the wedding."

Rose's face transformed before my eyes. Her worry and fear were replaced by a smile and joyous tears. I was blown away by the quick change in her demeanor. I grabbed her, and we hugged as I whispered in her ear, "You are the love of his life. Love doesn't die."

The next few hours were something of a blur. I ran around the room like I had jets on and connected table after table with their deceased loved ones. In between the serious messages sent, I used light-hearted humor to raise the energy in the room and keep everyone involved and connected.

I closed the event with a guided meditation to help those I couldn't connect to their loved ones in another way. Afterward, I stood by the exit and hugged people on their way out. Standing there, I really took in the mood change from the beginning of the event to the end; it was phenomenal. Each audience member seemed to walk with a little more bounce in their step and appeared a little bit lighter. Rose, the woman whose husband passed in the explosion, fell into my arms. She whispered in my ear, "Thank you. I can move forward now."

Those who had avoided all eye contact with me earlier, now waved and smiled. Others who came in with their heads hung low, fighting tears and fear, left laughing out loud and hugging one another.

I witnessed something amazing that night. Laughter trumped fear, and the room came alive with spirits, love, and the most unique family reunion I'd ever encountered.

I received hundreds of e-mails from those who had been present and others who had heard about the event. The money raised enabled me to bring on several practitioners to join me in helping the sick through my foundation.

Over the next few years, after that first experience with stage mediumship, local Boston news stations and FM radio stations began calling to request interviews or have me on as a guest. A half dozen newspapers took notice of the "soccer mom who talks to the dead." I never advertised and strictly relied on word of mouth. My mailing list soon grew to more than 10,000 people.

Today, I host events for audiences ranging from fifty people to five hundred. Once an event is listed on my website, it usually sells out within a couple of weeks, strictly through word of mouth and my website. My manager, Kelly, once got a call from a woman who sounded desperate to get a few tickets to a show. There was a constant "beep . . . beep . . . beep" in the background. Kelly asked, "What's that beeping sound?"

The woman whispered, "I'm a surgical nurse and I'm calling you from the operating room. That's just the heart monitor."

One of my favorite places to do readings is a quaint little inn on the water near Cape Cod. The Kinsale Inn in Mattapoisett, Massachusetts, is said to be haunted by the spirit of a well-known fishing captain. On numerous occasions, I could hear his heavy footsteps above me as I invited the spirits to come in. I'd worked this room a hundred times before, but the energy on one particular night in August was magnified. A chill ran up the back of my spine as I grabbed the microphone. I could feel the anticipation as I entered the room.

I did my usual explanation of how I work—"I hear them, feel how they passed, and see images. The information comes in quickly and I have to interpret the information so it makes sense."

I always like to share a particular reading at the beginning of each show to demonstrate how tricky interpreting what I am hearing and seeing can be. Sometimes my interpretation can be a bit off. During this particular reading, I was performing for a small gathering of thirty people at a yoga center. One woman's departed husband kept showing me a donkey in my mind's eye. I couldn't understand why.

"I'm seeing a donkey. Did you grow up in a farm town?" I asked her.

"No," she said, with a knowing grin.

"Maybe you had a pet mule?" I asked, reaching for a connection.

She shook her head no, a slight smile playing on her lips.

I was getting a little frustrated. *What's with the donkey?* I kept wondering. Then, a name came through. "I'm hearing George. Who is George?" I asked.

The woman jumped from her seat—all four feet, eleven inches of her. With a flushed face she blurted, "George, that jackass, is my husband!"

Joyful tears streamed down her face as she elaborated. "Every year for his birthday, I baked him a donkey-shaped cake, and I'd wear a T-shirt with an arrow pointing his way that said I'm with Jackass."

The crowd went wild, and the heaviness in the room melted into lightheartedness. Laughter takes the edge off this intense subject matter and helps the audience members let down their defenses. And I am able to make profound connections that allow us to celebrate life and enjoy a unique family reunion.

As I walked around the Kinsale Inn that August night—waiting for the spirits to slow down their vibrations so I could hear more clearly—I felt the spirit of a little girl trying to come through. "My mom is here, my mom is here!" she said louder and louder.

I felt drawn to a tall, slim blonde woman sitting at a table with seven others. Little did I know that the next ten minutes would change my life in ways I could never imagine. I received an e-mail from this little angel's mom, Gretchan, after the reading, which describes in detail our connection to the most amazing, powerful spirit I've ever had the privilege to bring through. I usually only remember bits and pieces of a reading, so I'm sharing Gretchan Pyne's account of our time together.

Maureen's events are always sold out too far in advance for me to plan. I wanted to attend over a year ago and finally got my chance when my husband's cousin, Linda, asked, "Hey, I have an extra ticket to see Maureen Hancock. Would you like to go?"

Just like that, we were there. My mother-in-law, father in-law, Linda, her sisters, and her mother sat around our table of eight—dead center.

It's amazing how anxious you feel while waiting for Maureen to start her show. My heart rate was slightly elevated, my palms a bit clammy. I wondered if everyone felt the same way. Maureen entered the room with her bottle of water. She reminded me immediately of a little pixie—blonde and bubbly. The dining room of the old historic inn was filled.

The first table she went to, Maureen had a couple stand up. She grabbed their hands and the magic began. She told them of her massive headache, the loud crashing noise, the smell of pavement. She told them that their son was there. He had died from massive head trauma received in a motorcycle accident . . . She was dead on!

Maureen continued to circle the room—table after table, person after person, more and more spirits coming through. Her accuracy is astounding. All the while Maureen somehow manages to weave in humor, grace, and unconditional love.

I could see her glancing over to our table throughout the first half hour. I tried to remain calm, wondering if she was picking up on my special little angel girl. I have moments when I can feel her with me, so pure and so powerful that I feel as though my heart will burst. She was with me that night. Maureen went to another table.

She finished her reading, turned around, and looked right at me from across the room. She rushed over and grabbed my trembling hand. With her eyes closed, she kept saying, "Slow it down. Slow it down." I knew whom she was talking to! You could almost see the energy soaring through her. Her eyes popped open—she looked straight into my eyes and exclaimed, "Lulu."

I didn't move . . . I couldn't move.

Maureen began to take on Lulu's mannerisms, her personality— giggly, excited, and full of energy. "I have to slow her down. She is so excited. She is so powerful and strong. She is so excited that you're here! She keeps saying, "My mommy is here. My mommy is here."

Maureen took a long deep breath, looked out the window, and

pointed to a short, gray fence by a gazebo in the park across the street from the inn. "Oh . . . she died outside . . . her heart . . . something fell on her. Her heart was crushed . . . a bicycle rack."

I didn't move . . . I couldn't move.

Maureen explained that Lulu is helping children who have passed and children who are still here. "That is what you do, too," she said. "You help children. What about Rose? I keep hearing something about Rose." Someone at our table shouted out, "Lulu's Rose-Colored Glasses!" Maureen brought the microphone back over to me.

I said, "I write children's books. *Lulu's Rose-Colored Glasses* is the first book.

Maureen explained that Lulu is a highly evolved being who served her purpose here on earth and now is able to help so many more. Maureen looked at me and said, "But you already know that."

I nodded my head. "I know, I know." It just felt like "being home" to experience someone else experiencing Lulu. Sharing openly, with Maureen, the immense joy and love that is Lulu, filled my heart beyond words.

After I brought through Lulu for Gretchan, her daughter's spirit stayed with me for days. She helped me connect several parents with their children who have passed and does so to this day. I consider Lulu my special angel and teacher. Gretchan continues to spread her message of love and hope to other parents: cherish every moment with your children, and stop along the way to see the world through rose-colored glasses.

This is the actual account of what happened to little Lulu:

On a hot summer day in July 2001, the Pyne family visited a local ice cream stand while vacationing on Cape Cod, Massachusetts. As four-year-old Lulu danced in the rain outside the stand, Warren, her dad, videotaped her posing in front of a metal bike rack. As she pointed to the beautiful double rainbow forming behind her, the bike rack—which was not chained to the ground—fell on little Lulu and severed her heart. Time stood still for the Pynes as Lulu danced across the rainbow to heaven.

My second son, Drew—another "miracle" baby—was born on July 22, 2001. Toward the end of August 2001, I began to have disturbing dreams of planes crashing into a building. In the past, I'd also dreamed of plane crashes that came to pass in real life within a few weeks. I'd even dreamt of John Kennedy Jr. crashing his Cessna and had shared it with my husband. When I told Greg about these new dreams, he couldn't just shrug them off, and we were both anxious and worried. I'm not sure what the purpose of the dreams was other than to add another element to my sensitivities. I wished the spirits gave me more information so that I could warn someone about upcoming events that might be avoided. Maybe that will come as my abilities expand even more.

On September 11, 2001, I woke up sick to my stomach. I couldn't stop vomiting. My anxiety was in full throttle. A voice in my head told me to turn on the television. It was just after 9 AM. A plane had crashed into the World Trade Center in New York City. I immediately reached for the phone and called my husband. While we were on the phone, the second plane hit the other tower. Paralyzed by shock, we ended the conversation. Later, we lived and relived the horrors of the coming days.

Being at Logan Airport after the tragedy was beyond miserable. My office overlooked the Terminal B tarmac from which the hijacked planes had taken off. Armed guards marched around the office, and it was as if a dark cloud of death loomed overhead. At the end of the workday, I'd literally run from my office to the shuttle boat in fear of a bomb or plane crash.

I could no longer watch the television coverage of the disaster and the replays of the towers falling. The chilling voices of the victims calling out from beyond overwhelmed me. If a picture of someone flashed on the television screen, I would hear in my head, *Oh, my poor family. Please help them.* Or, I would be consumed with a heavy feeling of sadness, and I would cry for hours at a time in great despair. I prayed every morning for the victims and their families. Finally, about three months after 9/11, the voices of the victims stopped haunting me and almost completely stopped. I believe for many of these spirits, the transition to the other side took some time. They had to get used to their new spirit bodies and learn ways to communicate with those left behind. I prayed for healing for the family members left behind, and for peace for those who had passed.

I started doing free readings for the widows and other survivors of 9/11. One of my clients, who is now a friend, brought her children in to see me so they could gain some comfort after their father, Jeffrey Coombs, passed on American Airlines Flight 11, which hit the North

Tower of the World Trade Center. Their dad asked me to address each child and talk about things going on in their lives at that time, so they would know he was not missing out on their lives. He talked about a recent soccer tournament in which the daughter received a trophy. (When I'm communicating with spirits, I mostly *hear* their messages as they come in. My strongest ability is called clairaudience [hearing the spirits].)

Whether I am doing a spirit reading or hands-on healing, each case I see is different and must be handled in its own unique way and with extreme compassion. For example, Donna is a forty-year-old mother of twin twelve-year-old girls. Her lung cancer returned after being in remission for a few years. When I first saw her, it had traveled through her lymph nodes, bones, and brain. Her strength and will to live always takes my breath away. When I arrived for our first visit, she asked a very strange question: "You're not going to burp on me are you?"

"Uh, no, I don't think I'll be doing that today. Why do you ask?" I said with a grin.

"Well, my friends pitched in and had a healer come to the house the other day. He kept waving his hands over my body and burping loudly. He said he was pulling the dark entities out of me."

"I can assure you I won't be expelling from either end today, and I don't see any goblins hanging around you," I calmly explained.

Donna expressed her sorrow and fear at the thought of having to leave her daughters. "Hannah and Haley were lying next to me last night begging me not to leave them. They said they couldn't live without their mother. It broke my heart to hear them talk about me missing out on their lives . . . graduations, weddings, and babies."

I grabbed her hands and looked her in the eyes. "You will *not* miss out on their lives. I promise you, you'll be a part of their lives, guiding them and sending them signs to let them know you are right by their sides. I will talk to them and help them understand death. And I'll give them the tools they need to be aware of your presence. Love doesn't die, Donna."

We gathered around the fireplace in Donna's living room two days later. The girls seemed anxious about what I would tell them. Hannah fidgeted in her seat as Haley bit her nails.

"Death is not the end," I explained. "This physical body is like a vehicle that drives us around. When your mom's vehicle breaks down, she will step out of it and continue on. You will feel her all around you. Talk to her as if she is still here, even if you just speak to her in your head. She will come to you in dreams, talk to you through music, and she will find ways to let you know she is always with you."

"Will my mother still be in pain when she dies? asked Hannah. "Will she always be sleeping?" (Donna slept a great deal of the time because of the pain medication she was on.)

"No," I answered. "She will be completely out of pain and able to breathe again. She will have all her energy back and be just like she was before she got sick. Her smile will be bigger than ever because she will be able to see you both."

I could see their anxieties just melt in front of my eyes. Before we finished our session, I gave them each a pink journal with a big purple heart on the front. "Use this to write down your feelings and whatever is on your mind."

Journaling is a tool I suggest to my clients to help them through the process of a loved one passing and their own grief. It's especially helpful for children who may not have an outlet to express their feelings.

Before we hugged good-bye, Donna pulled herself up off the couch and, dragging her oxygen tank behind her, leaned over and whispered in my ear, "I'm not afraid to leave them now. I know I won't really be gone. I was so afraid there would be just darkness when I passed. Over the years, and through my own journey to understand life after death, I have experienced so many miracles and events that have cemented my belief in an afterlife. I have read hundreds of books on the subject of death, dying, and the afterlife. It's much more powerful to experience evidence of an afterlife rather than just read about it—I've done both.

Thankfully, I started down this pathway with a strong faith in God. To me, God is nonphysical. But even though I can't see him, I trust he is present and can hear me. Spirit loved ones also may not be physically present, but that doesn't mean they don't exist. (Just as the sun's power and energy is always there, even when it's hidden by clouds.) Science has taught us that energy can't die. And we are all made up of energy.

I have been blessed to be a witness to so many physical passings. When you are a witness to such an intense event, it's hard not to feel the presence of a higher power. I've actually witnessed those on the threshold of crossing over—reaching their hands out, smiling, and calling the name of the person who is there to greet them. Many look as though they actually see a familiar family member who has gone home before them (or physically passed). I too can feel the presence of spirit and hear them give messages to those in the room—especially the person about to pass.

I have had conversations with countless spirits and the final message to those left behind is always similar: I'm okay. You'll be okay. And I'll see you again.

I'm not here to convince anyone that there is an afterlife, but I do hope through my own faith, experiences, and interactions with the living and dead that I've planted seeds of hope and possibilities that there is something more out there when we leave this earth. I help those left behind to see death differently—which helps them to live life differently. My job is to help those suffering and left behind.

My cancer clients range from infants to centenarians. When I enter the presence of the sick, I gently lay my hands on them and offer prayers of comfort for their weak outer shells and prayers of peace for their journey home. The question I hear most from the dying is, "Who will be there to greet me?" Then my answers flow as I list the names of their loved ones who are waiting to embrace them on the other side.

I feel so blessed to be an "overseas operator" with a direct line to heaven. As my clients relax into their newfound peace, embracing their next phase of existence, I salute their courage and am humbled to be a witness to this beautiful transition.

⚬⚬

Do you ever sense that you have a gift, a talent that you'd like to share with the world? Perhaps it was something that you loved to do as a child or that you knew you'd always be good at, even if you didn't understand why? Maybe it was working with animals or with children or being an artist. Whatever your gift is, have you said yes to it yet? Saying yes to a gift can sometimes be scary. *What will other people say? I can't make money at that! What if I get rejected? I'm not good enough to do that for other people! I'm too old* . . . blah, blah, blah—the list could go on forever, don't you agree?

Regardless of your fearful thoughts, your talent never goes away. It is waiting to realize its full expression through you. Instead of thinking of all the ways to say, "No, I can't do it," stop and think about all the reasons to say yes to your gift. Consider the following:

1. What is the dream hidden in your heart? What is the passion hidden in your soul? What wants to dance its way into being?
2. List all the reasons/excuses (aka fears) that you've given yourself that keep you from sharing your gift.
3. Notice how you feel when you write down all these negative reasons. Pretty crappy, huh? How does this negativity make you feel?
4. Now, take a moment and imagine yourself sharing this gift easily and effortlessly. Feel it. Breathe it in. Dare yourself to stretch out of your comfort zone, and give yourself per-

mission to come up with as many reasons as you can
to make your gift or talent a reality.

5. Notice how you feel when you write down all the positive
   reasons to say yes to your gift. How do these reasons
   to say yes make you feel? Feels pretty good, huh?

6. Choose to focus on feeling good, and your new attitude
   will help attract positive, meaningful changes in your
   life, helping you to bring your dream to life.

7. Say yes to your gift each day.

5

Sean Michael— Tragedy to Triumph

Preparing to leave for a small Postcards from Heaven event, I was running around the house gathering my things. I was nearly out of my mind trying to locate my makeup bag. Since I was running late, I'd planned to apply my makeup in the car at the red lights.

Drew, my three-year-old, pulled at my pant leg. "Mommy, don't go," he cried, tears streaming down his face.

I picked him up in my arms, kissed away his tears, and said, "Daddy will be here any minute."

"I want Mommy," he insisted, and began crying again, louder this time.

Just then the phone rang. I could barely make out the voice on the other end as I strained to hear over Drew's sobs. Leeann, the receptionist at my office, said in a quiet, shaking voice, "Maureen, the Middleboro police are here looking for your sister Rose."

Do we owe the town taxes? I wondered. *Why would they pick on small fries like us?*

Next I heard a male voice. "This is Officer Santos. We're looking for your sister, Rose Ewas."

My psychic antenna was down, and I couldn't understand the urgency in his voice. His next words will echo in my head and heart for the rest of my days: "Her son, Sean, is deceased. We need to let her know."

For that split second I did not speak English. I couldn't comprehend his words. *What does "deceased" mean? Oh right, deceased, dead people . . . the people that bombard me all day long with messages for their loved ones.*

"Sean?"

Time stopped.

Can I fix this? Can I reverse this? No. Our precious Sean Michael is gone.

The officer refused to tell me what happened over the phone. I hung up and immediately saw Sean, my nineteen-year-old nephew, in my mind's eye, lying under his car in the third bay of his father's shop—a shipping container warehouse. Something went horribly wrong as he worked on his dream Mustang. He showed me the scene and showed me that he'd left his body before he knew what hit him.

At that moment, my husband walked in the door, returning from the warehouse. I yelled to him but no sound came out. It was like one of those dreams where someone is chasing you or trying to kill you and you can't get your voice to work. You try with all your might to yell, part of you knowing you are in a dream and will wake up. But I was very much awake.

My voice cracked as I screamed, "Where was Sean when you left? Was he under his car? Was he under his car?!"

Greg stood at the bottom of the stairs. I stared down at him with my baby in my arms, clinging to him for dear life.

"Yes, he was under his car when I just left him. He was trying to cut something with some saw."

I needed to know if Greg had said good-bye to Sean. Despite my pain, I felt if he had said good-bye to Sean we would all be okay.

"Yes, I said bye and asked if he needed anything. He said no. Why?"

I couldn't get the words out clearly enough for him to hear. Greg stood there with a perplexed look.

I said it again. "He's dead . . . he's dead . . . Sean is dead!"

This wasn't supposed to happen. In my line of work, I deal with death on a daily basis. But tragedy was never supposed to strike my family or anyone I was close with. On that balmy March day, however, death happened to my family.

I ran around the house in a panic, trying to remember what I needed to do next. Oh, yes, I told the cop not to tell my sister until I got there. I needed to be the one to tell her. I called to cancel my show.

The drive to my sister's house seemed like hours. I felt like someone was pushing their knees into my back from the backseat of the car. Somebody wanted my attention. It was Sean! He was in the car with me, telling me how to break the news to his mother. He said he was fine, and my mother's mom, Grammy Mac, had come down to take him home. He was not afraid and acted like his cool laid-back self.

I had to tell someone before I lost it completely. I called my mother— the rock of Gibraltar. I knew she would help me get there and give me the strength and guidance I needed to do what I had to do. The phone rang about five times. I was screaming out loud, "Pick up the phone. Please be home!" She answered with a shaky voice. It was as if she knew something already. "Mom?" I asked.

"Who died?" she snapped. That's how our crazy psychic family works —at times teetering on psychotic.

I asked if she was sitting down. When she confirmed that she was, I said, "Sean passed away."

We don't like to use the word "dead" in my family. We all agree that nobody really "dies," they just "go home." I filled her in and she said nothing at first. Then she quickly declared, "I'll call everyone and we'll be right there."

I finally arrived at my sister's Victorian home. The sky was eerily magnificent, with pink and purple hues. Although it was the beginning of March, Sean's day of passing was comfortably warm. Still, I was numb. Ironically, the day Sean passed was the twelve-year anniversary of my life-altering car accident. I pulled up behind a black SUV, jumped out of the car, and approached the two officers.

I looked at the older of the two cops and said, "His car fell on him."

The men glanced at each another as if I'd been spying on them. A worried look came over the younger cop's face. "How would you know that?" he asked. "The case is under investigation. We haven't released that information."

Trying not to sound like I was putting them on, I just said, "It's what I do. I talk to the dead." There's just no sugar coating it.

As we walked up the driveway, I felt strangely calm. "Get ready, you have no idea how she's going to react," I warned the officers, preparing them for a passionate wild woman who'd spent her entire life sacrificing her own happiness for her precious children.

Ringing my sister's bell to break this news felt surreal, like a dream from which I wanted desperately to wake up. Rosie came down the stairs in a towel. She'd been in the shower so she hadn't heard them knocking earlier. That was a small miracle that I know Sean arranged. It was better, much better, for me to break the news to my sister.

I was screaming to myself, *How am I going to tell my sister her baby is gone?! Why do I have to be the person to tell her?!* I knew why. For the past few months, Sean and I had been sitting together each afternoon and watching *Crossing Over* with John Edward, a popular New York medium. We would talk about death and dying. I believe on some soul level Sean knew he would live to be nineteen and then journey on after fulfilling his soul contract.

I wish Sean had prepared me for the blood-curdling screams that would come from the depths of my sister's soul in the next few moments. Rosie looked at me and I knew she knew something was terribly wrong.

She fell down the last two stairs in her hallway and grabbed for my arm. She squeezed it hard and asked, "What's wrong, who is it?"

I could feel my lips moving, but I can't remember exactly what was said. I think it went something like this . . . "It's Sean. There's been an accident."

Rosie was frantically looking at me and then over my shoulder at the cops. There was panic in her voice as she asked, "Is he okay, is he okay? What happened, what happened?"

Her whole body was shaking as she fell into my arms. I know she knew he was gone.

Through my tears I said, "His car fell on him. Grammy came to get him. He's okay."

Rosie thought I meant he was okay as in still alive. I had to reach deep into the depths of my soul to speak the next sentence: "He's gone, Rosie. Sean's an angel now. He's with Grammy Mac in heaven."

Rosie let go like a wounded animal. Her primal cry filled the hall and spilled out onto the side porch. She grabbed Officer Santos's shirt and almost lifted him off his feet.

"No, no, no," she kept screaming and screaming, filling the neighborhood with her pain, her worst fear realized. Rosie reached her arms up to the sky to let out a deep, moaning roar—emptying her essence and all that she used to be. Then she collapsed into my arms as I helped her back into the house.

There were so many thoughts running through my mind. Sean's dad was in China. How would we tell him? His sister, Stassia, would be home soon. Telling her would be just as hard as telling Rosie. Stassia and Sean were best friends. The phone rang. It was Stassia. She is very intuitive and has done some spirit readings with me. She knew something was not right.

"What's going on . . . did something happen? I'm getting a weird feeling," she said.

"There's been an accident. Sean was in an accident." I replied.

Stassia's pitch heightened. "What hospital is he in? I'm on the highway. I'll meet you there."

At this point I knew I just had to get her home. If I told her Sean had gone to heaven over the phone she would not be able to drive. I told her to come home and we would all go together. She kept asking if he was okay. I said I didn't know yet.

A few minutes later, Stassia came running into the house. When she saw the two officers standing in the hallway, she fell to her knees whimpering. "No, no, no!" She knew without actually hearing the news.

Sean had already been taken to the Massachusetts medical examiner's office in Boston. Rosie couldn't understand why he needed to go there. One of the cops whispered in my ear that they were required by law to investigate and do an autopsy to rule out foul play. Rosie couldn't bear the thought of her baby being alone in a cold hallway waiting for what could be days for the autopsy, not to mention what they would have to do to him.

Within an hour, my mother and I had made dozens of calls and word spread quickly. Groups of family members and friends started pouring into the old Victorian on Webster Street in the quaint farm town of Middleboro. With each ring of the doorbell came different pitches of crying, yelling, and moans.

Eventually I took refuge upstairs because I thought I would lose my mind. I couldn't begin to imagine how Rosie remained sane. She wrapped herself in Sean's dark-blue fluffy North Face jacket, a special Christmas gift he'd received, and covered her legs with blankets from his bed as she huddled on the living room couch sobbing.

I made the call to the hotel room in Singapore where John, Sean's dad, was staying. I tried my best to communicate to the receptionist that I wanted them to wake him up so he could make the next flight out.

He called home when he landed in Chicago for a layover. I yelled, "Be quiet, John's calling!"

"Hey, what's up?" he said. "I'll be landing in Boston about nine tonight. Where's Rosie? Put her on the phone," John said. I took a deep breath and put on the best acting job of my life.

"The Expedition had a flat tire, so she's down the street."

"Call Sean to go fix it for her. I keep trying to reach him and he's not answering his cell phone," John stated.

"He's down there helping her, so he probably doesn't hear his phone," I said.

"He did such an awesome job running my business while I was gone. He's really coming into his own. I think I'll have him take it over some day," he proudly boasted. "Tell Sean to get off his ass and help his mother and I'll see you guys tonight. Who's picking me up?"

"A few of us will come in to Logan to get you," I said.

"Good, we'll grab a late dinner at Sol Azteca in Brookline," John said happily.

I tapped into my old connections at Logan Airport to arrange a private meeting room off the gate to tell John his only son was gone. We loaded ourselves into two cars and headed into Boston. The radio played softly in the background. I thought I was the only one who noticed every song that came on seemed like a message from beyond.

First, "Calling All Angels" by Train came on. Each word in every song to follow seemed as if Sean spoke directly to this living band of angels off to do a job. Spirits often use music to communicate to the living. Just the right song might come on when you're thinking of them, and the words seem to speak to you.

At the airport, it felt like waiting for someone to finally come through the door at a surprise party, only this was the worst surprise anyone could ever walk into. We were afraid John would collapse after flying more than twenty-four hours and hearing the news. An ambulance waited just in case, and two EMTs stood by the gate. You see, on the outside John is the Marlboro man with a tough exterior, yet he weeps like a baby at weddings and Kodak commercials.

Rosie walked out of the holding room and I followed. She went up to John and just fell in his arms sobbing. He saw all of us standing around waiting for him.

His face turned pale. "Oh my God, your mother died, didn't she?"

Rosie just kept shaking her head back and forth saying, "No."

Our mother Grace Agnes has nine lives. She has flatlined and come back more times than Bob in the movie *Groundhog Day.*

Rosie grabbed John's shoulders and looked him in the eye saying, "It's Sean. There's been an accident."

It was as if a 300-pound gorilla wound up and punched John in the gut. He wanted the facts and wanted them fast. He lit up a cigarette in the nonsmoking terminal as we all took turns hugging him.

When we got back to the house, John needed to go to the shop where it all went down. Greg and I went with him. There were already dozens of flowers and writings on the wall—a makeshift memorial for Sean from his friends and family.

When I walked out back to the bays, I could see Sean's dream car, a white Mustang, up on cinder blocks. His sneakers were in front of the car. I could feel him watching us. When I looked over at Sean's black Mustang—his first car—in the middle bay, I saw a face through the windshield. I gasped. I knew it was Sean. He smiled. John walked up behind me. At that moment, a foggy shadow formed the shape of a smiley face on the windshield of the black Mustang, which remains there to this day. We also noticed that the number 222 was written in dust. Little did we know that Sean would use this number as a symbol of his presence for years to come.

"You know, I told Sean I loved him and he said it back to me a couple of days ago. I told him my customers said he did a great job. He really stepped up to the plate," John said quietly, as he rifled through Sean's notes on the desk.

After a few rough teenage years, Sean and his dad had started to bond again. In those last few days before Sean fulfilled his soul contract here, it was as if they both knew something momentous was about to happen. Maybe they knew on some level deeper than everyday consciousness.

I do believe that the soul knows on some higher level when its journey ends. Some victims of 9/11 prepared wills just days before that tragic event. There truly are no accidents. I am told this repeatedly by those in the spirit world. As hard as it was for my family to understand at the time, we now embrace that Sean's agreement was to be here on this earth for nineteen years. He even filled me in from the spirit world recently to say that he got two extra years. He wrapped his car around a pole at seventeen and should not have survived that accident. Leave it to Sean to broker a deal with God.

Sean touched so many lives in his short time here and continues to be our teacher. He showed his entire family that we don't die. We merely drive a rented vehicle—the outer shell of our essence—until the lease is up.

Here's a love letter about loving and letting go from Rosie's heart to yours:

Losing a child is like dying, except you find you still walk the earth. Six years after my son physically passed, and after five years of facilitating grief groups for parents, I still see and feel the aftereffects of his passing, but now I experience them a little differently. I believed, like many parents, that I would never smile again, let alone laugh, and wondered why the world didn't "get it." Never for the life of me did I think that one day I not only would survive this but that I would, and do, thrive.

Let me give you a little background from the beginning, lest you think this was in any way less than heart-and-soul rendering. I, in fact, felt destroyed when Sean passed. My image of myself was broken into a million pieces, lying shattered on the ground. I begged and threatened God to "release me" . . . to let me see for myself that my child was okay . . . to release me from my body so that I did not have to feel this unbearable agony. I wanted to hurt God, like he had hurt me. Thankfully, I no longer feel that way, and most days I am more than grateful for my life and my everyday existence. I'd like to share with you the ways that I began to see the light of day. It all stared with a cup of tea.

Sitting with my dear friend Lorna one day in the months following Sean's physical passing, I realized I was enjoying a cup of tea. I
couldn't have been more surprised. I even said in shock, "I'm enjoying
this . . . it tastes . . . good."

Then, one day, I put on lipstick, even though I still did not want to
smile. These small little victories were the beginning for me.

We all tend to grieve differently, although there are many similarities
in grief, and some "lucky ones" even go straight through the process.
But for most of us, feeling it all, sometimes breaking the day into bits—
one morning, or afternoon or sometimes one hour at a time, is all you
can handle. It takes everything you have to keep living. And many of
us survive in spite of ourselves. Let me share now some of the bigger
steps I took to come back, to be the "new me." Perhaps you can hold
on to them like a lifeline, as I did.

To begin with, I let people help me. This was a position I was
not very familiar with. I was used to being in the role of helping
other people. Grieving is so exhausting that I just let people do things
for me. *You want to cook me dinner?* Great. *You want to take me out to
breakfast?* Fine. *Let me sob wildly and wretchedly in your presence?*
You are going to heaven.

There is no road map for this horrid landscape . . . grieving a child.
So, you must make your own.

I've told my parents' groups that in my opinion, if you did not pass
with your child, then you are here for a reason—your soul contract is
not up. So now what? If I had all the answers, I'd share them. In this
case, you must live it out, little by little. Find your new way and the
new you just by putting one foot in front of the other. Try to have faith
that one day you will feel peace again. I know it's possible! I believe it's

imperative to look for every conceivable way to find hope, then to hold on to that for dear life . . . because it will save you.

To try to find meaning again in this bleak new world takes courage. This is not for the fainthearted because it can be grueling. One step forward and then sometimes two steps back. I'm saying this not to discourage you but to give you the fortitude that you will need. If I and countless other parents can survive this, then you can too.

In the beginning, I learned to stay away from books, people, and organizations that made me feel worse. I can distinctly remember throwing a grief self-help book that disturbed me across my living room. And then, even *that* was not enough. I picked up the book, went to the door, and threw it outside. I was raw and vulnerable, and I learned to protect myself.

It was in this protective mode that many wonderful ways of living a richer life slowly developed. Protecting myself meant that I made darn sure I got plenty of sleep—in fact, lots and lots of it. I watch my sleep habits even now, because if I do not, I'm sure to be in for a weepy day. It was here as well, that I began to take a stand for myself in the light of others' well-meaning comments. If I wanted to sleep, I did. If I wanted to stay in my pajamas longer or get in them sooner than was sociably acceptable, I did. Frankly, I no longer cared what people thought of me.

Everything was unfolding in an organic, especially quiet way. *I* became especially quiet. I had been trying to get a "bead" on God since I was a child, and now I found the old ways did not cut it. So, I developed my own contemplative ritual—a spiritual part of my day that sustained and held me up. In my darkest hours, this kept my heart beating.

Also, believe it or not, another great way I found to support myself was by eating very well and taking top-grade supplements. If my body was not functioning well, then that was going to be another burden.

When I was ready, I began to think of ways that would inspire me somehow to want to live life to the fullest. At first, the only way I could make myself do that was to do it in honor of Sean. Everything I did in the beginning was for Sean. Just two and half months before Sean passed, he gave me a book called *Living Out Loud*, about getting out into the world and having a creative life, and that's what I worked toward. I could feel him rooting for me and I did not want to disappoint him!

My first foray into the world, again in honor of Sean, was taking a course at a peaceful yoga and workshop center in the Berkshires of Massachusetts called Kripalu. It was one of the hardest things I have ever done in my life. I took a big leap of faith and went by myself when I was still very raw. I spent a good deal of the time there in tears. In the classroom, dining room, Jacuzzi, bed . . . you name it. I was a mess. But I did it and was better for it. It propelled me back out into the world and got me thinking about how I might be of help. I thought if I was going to be here anyway, why not do something to make the world a better place?

Kripalu became my spiritual home for several years. It was a beacon of light for me to escape to from time to time. I think we all need to find those places that are refuges or sanctuaries. Our soul is always talking to us, especially in the dark nights. Listen. Listen with your broken heart wide open and let in all the hope that you can muster. I promise you this, you will be with your child again, and if you cannot hold on to that truth yet, I will hold it for you.

Blessings and peace to you dear, dear soul,

Rosie Dalton Ewas

Sean's passing was so tragic and unexpected. And as with any tragedy, we never thought it could happen to our family. But it did, and we have become closer because of it. Rosie and I touch base a few times a day and always make time to see one another. Stassia has recently embraced her gift of spirit communication and is a practicing medium. She says Sean is her guide, and he is assisting her in helping many people heal after the loss of a loved one. Rosie made it a point to spread her knowledge of life everlasting to other parents who have lost a child. For the past five years, she has facilitated a support group. Grieving will be a lifelong process for my sister, but through it all, she has found a shimmering light—a glimmer of hope.

❧

While hearing a message from a medium can be very healing, and can bring a tremendous amount of comfort to you, here are other ways to help you through the grieving process.

When you lose someone you love, it can feel like you've just landed in a foreign country, and you're not quite sure where you are. Your surroundings may feel different, you may feel that the people around you don't understand you, that food doesn't taste the same, that you can't relate to people, and you just want to go "home." Your body and your mind may have been through a lot. No matter how much preparation you had before your loved one's death, things will feel different. Be gentle with yourself.

There are many paths of grief, and everyone moves through it at their own pace, and in their own way. Just as no two snowflakes are alike, no two people will grieve the same way. Some need to talk about it, others don't. Some will hang on to a loved one's clothing and belongings for years; others feel the need to distribute it right away. Please don't judge how someone moves through their grief. They are dancing through their own delicate journey.

Also, recognize that on some days you may feel like you're doing really well, and then a few days later have a setback. That is perfectly normal. Any little reminder might trigger a pocket of sadness: someone mentioning your loved one's name, a song that you hear, seeing their name on a piece of mail, a piece of sad news on TV. And just when you thought you had a handle on things, you find yourself in a puddle of tears. It can happen anywhere, anytime. So, carry some tissues with you, know that you're not alone, and don't feel that you have to apologize to anyone.

When you are feeling better, please don't feel guilty for not being sad. Your loved ones in spirit want you to feel good again. They want you to feel peace. And feeling some joy again does not mean you'll ever forget them, nor does it mean that you don't care. The love you had for them and the love they had for you lives forever in your heart. That never dies.

6

I'm Not Dead—
I'm Different

After my nephew Sean passed, my sister Rosie and I decided to work together to help other parents learn what our grief and healing journey had taught us. I stopped giving private readings for the public in 2004, leaving behind a two-year waiting list. Word quickly spread that I was now dedicating my time to providing free, private family sessions for parents with children in heaven. The response overwhelmed me: upward of fifteen to twenty requests came in per week, and my waiting list grew to more than 350 parents. I was forced to narrow the guidelines for a free reading, and I limited my readings to children who had recently passed (within one year) and were under thirty. But things don't always go as we've planned.

While working late one Friday evening, I received a call from a woman. My eyes burned as I rested my head on the desk. I felt completely spent after a full day of spirits. I toyed with letting the machine answer the call, but a gentle voice in my head nudged me to pick up the receiver. I'm sure glad I listened.

"Maureen, this is Evelyn. I heard you do free readings for parents who have lost a child," said the woman.

"Yes, I do," I replied.

Her voice wavered as she softly spoke these words: "My oldest son, Charles, recently passed. He was my pride and joy. I miss him so much. I just need to know that he's okay and with my husband in heaven. Can you please help?"

"I'm sorry, Evelyn," I responded. "I'm sure he *is* with your husband and out of pain. How old was your son?"

"Sixty-seven."

I paused for a moment and took a deep breath. I looked down at my parent waiting list and the names of the many children who had gone home to heaven:

Jayden, 10, killed when a snowblower snagged the hood on her coat.

Alexa, 19, died in a car accident coming home from a country fest concert.

Jimmy, 17, electrocuted while holding a pole with his dad at a job site.

Sean, 9, killed while riding an ATV on a playdate with a friend.

On the other end of the phone line was a sweet, salt-of-the earth mother with labored breathing and paralyzing grief. I knew Evelyn was hoping and praying for a comforting message from "her boy." I'm against cloning, but for a moment I wished someone would take a piece of me (maybe from my muffin top), and let it sit in a petri dish to make a few more of me to go around. As gently as I could, I explained my predicament.

"I completely understand," said Evelyn, without a detectable trace of disappointment. Suddenly, the receiver picked up static.

"Can you hear that?" I asked.

"What is it?" replied Evelyn.

"I think it's your son trying to get our attention!"

A heavy sigh filled the airwaves.

"Evelyn, did Charles have congestive heart failure? He's telling me he was filled with fluid."

"Oh yes, he most certainly did. He told you that? He spoke to you?"

"Who is Joseph?" I asked.

After a long pause, Evelyn answered, "Joe was my husband. We were married for fifty-two years. He was the love of my life."

"Evelyn, this exchange has been so unexpected. I know your son orchestrated this so you can have peace knowing he's okay."

"I can feel him now," Evelyn whispered. "I'm holding his picture in my hands. You're not going to believe this, but it looks like his lips are moving. His eyes are shining and his smile just got bigger. Is this my imagination?"

"No, Evelyn. You are not imagining it. He's telling you he loves you. He's whole again."

"He had Down syndrome. He lived with me, and we did everything together. I found him dead in his bed three weeks ago. I needed to make sure someone else was taking care of him now. I'll finally be able to sleep tonight."

Evelyn taught me a profound lesson: a mother will always be a mother, no matter what age her children are. She will go to the ends of the earth to make sure her children are cared for, loved, cherished, and protected—even if they predecease her. The journey of motherhood never ends.

In those fragile days after Sean's physical death, Rosie spent most of her time in the safe haven of her bedroom. Some days she wrapped herself in a cocoon of blankets; on other days she sat up and read inspirational books, meditated, prayed, and journaled. She created a shrine on the antique table next to her bed and placed a photo of Sean there. This picture spoke to her, and at times his eyes appeared to be moving, following *her* movements. A brilliant bright white light circled his head. And on the rare occasions when Rosie laughed in the midst of her grieving, this light seemed to bounce off the photo, and Sean's smile grew bigger.

Many parents tell me that they feel guilty if they laugh or smile in the midst of their grief and mourning. But the children in heaven tell me they are "lifted up" when their parents experience moments of joy. Their spirit bodies are refueled, and their souls vibrate more intensely, so they can better connect and communicate with the living.

Rosie was able to turn her family's tragedy into triumph by channeling her grief into helping other parents who have lost a child. Despite her grief, which is present daily in different ways, Rosie made the commitment to pick herself up, bit by bit, slowly—very slowly at times—and she eventually began a local support group for parents with children in heaven.

It was amazing to watch Rosie—still healing herself— stand for the first time in the large workshop room at my office in front of fifty to sixty newly grieving parents. "Even though we can't physically hug them anymore," she said at that first workshop, "please trust they are here. Feel them, in your soul, as they wrap their arms around you and guide you. Listen to what they tell you, see how happy they appear, and know, please know, more than anything, that you will see them again."

I watched Rosie stand in front of hundreds of parents, month after month, while her own heart was still so tender, and speak about ways to get through the day, to get out of bed, to continue in this life without a *physical* connection with the children. Her work made me beam with pride. Her strength and ability to plant seeds of hope are nothing short of miraculous.

I met an amazing woman through the support group. Her name is Gail Hunter. In December 2006, her only daughter, Anjuli, passed in a car accident on her way to Maine to visit college friends during the winter. In June 2009, the unthinkable happened. Gail's only other living child, Drew, passed in a kayak accident in Colorado.

A friend of Gail's called to give me the news.

"I'm calling you from Colorado, Maureen. Gail Hunter's son, Drew, drowned in a horrible kayak accident. The services are today. Gail is going to need you."

I was stunned. I was in L.A. at the time filming a guest appearance on a new Fox talk show called *Wedlock or Deadlock*. As the busy cast and crew bustled around me—fitting microphones, adjusting lighting, applying makeup—my world froze. I imagined this mother losing both her children tragically. Leaning against the nearest wall for support, I wept.

Gail and I became fast friends after our first session to connect with her daughter, Anjuli. When I later asked Gail if our session had helped her, she insisted I read the part of her journal with the "Maureen" story. Gail asked me to share it with others so that another mother might gain strength. The following are actual excerpts from Gail Hunter's personal journal:

August 2, 2007

We're seeing Maureen Hancock tomorrow. I'm nervous, excited, and shaky. Jeremy [Gail's husband] is leery, and doesn't want to go, but he doesn't want to miss anything, either. Anjuli, please be there. Please give us a huge sign, something to let us know you are okay, that you are still with us. We both need it, but your father really is lost in his grief for you. My heart aches.

August 3, 2007

Where to begin? I am still in a daze. Jeremy, the skeptic, when asked by a friend, "What was it like?" replied, "I feel like I had an hour-long conversation with my daughter." How does Maureen do it? How did she totally get the essence of Anjuli? Maureen's gentle touch, her sense of humor, her beautiful smile, all helped us to be comfortable with this crazy experience. She totally "got" Anjuli's personality, her drive and confidence, her spirit. For over an hour, we sat transfixed by the accurate details she relayed, and the purity of her intent. I can't describe the feeling of *knowing* your daughter is there, *knowing* she is sending love and trying to communicate whatever she can to help us accept that it *is* her, so we could open our hearts and our minds.

Anjuli told us details of the accident that were unknown to either of us, but later confirmed. She mentioned a locket, but then corrected herself to say ten lockets. (We had given out ten lockets to her friends!)

For the first time since we lost you, Anjuli, I feel hope and really *believe* that we will once again be reunited. I'm determined to pay more attention to signs, to listen to that inner voice that says, "You are blessed to have had Anjuli for twenty-three years, to be her mother." I feel lifted up by all the angels that watch over me and work to lift my spirits.

I can't wait to tell Drew that she spoke of him, by name, and sent her love. She said to tell him she watches over him, like a hawk in the sky. How will he react to this? I wish he could have been at our meeting. Even when your head tells you no, your heart tells you yes.

June 18, 2009

Oh God, it cannot be. The worst thing imaginable can't have happened to us . . . again. Drew, our precious Drew, is dead—gone like Anjuli in the flash of an accident—a mere two and a half years after his sister. How can we live without our two children in this world?

I received this e-mail from Maureen: "I got your message and didn't want you to think I forgot about you. I was in California when I heard the news. I am here for you. I wanted to call you but it is late. I've been waiting for him to be ready. I can finally feel Drew tonight. As you can imagine, he was elated to see Anjuli, then looked back and said, "Oh crap." He is such a free spirit, an old soul. He was a bit pissed at him-self for getting stuck or something.

June 21, 2009

A phone call from Maureen, telling me Drew is bugging her to call me. Just hearing her voice is calming, though it starts my heart racing, knowing that she can give me a connection with Drew. We just left the memorial service and gathering, feeling weak and spent. Can this really happen over the phone? Can Maureen really connect me with Drew? She starts in, letting me know he is there, telling me details once again that were only known by those with him when he died in the kayaking accident. She gets the essence of Drew, totally—his per-sonality, the exact things he would say: "What happened? I had it all under control." And he did. And he would have said that, just that way. I am so thankful, because of everything that happened with Anjuli, that Drew and I talked about the afterlife. He didn't know what he believed, but saw the comfort we received from the messages Maureen gave us. He wrote in his journal in a message to his sister:

"I hope you are with me now, seeing what I see and feeling what I feel, so that my thoughts are somehow transferred to your spirit wher-ever it may be. Please help me to find the strength that I know you are sending Mom to help her find inner peace. I can only hope that I can live my life with as much passion and positive vibes that you showed and shared with so many friends and strangers. You brought people together and made them better people for knowing you. I love you, Anj."

In the span of time between losing Anjuli, and then Drew, Maureen and I have been connected in so many ways. After seeing Maureen, a friend took me to a taping of the John Edward show, where I got a reading. I stood there, looking completely idiotic, as I smiled the whole time he gave me my message. I was smiling because he confirmed everything Maureen had told us in our reading. Afterward, I just knew the reason I was there, getting a reading, was not only for me but also for the connections that would happen to help Maureen get her message out to a larger audience. When the John Edward staff came to film a follow-up segment at our house, much of my explanation of the "lightness" of my grief involved my meeting with Maureen.

The connections still reverberate between Maureen and me, like a spider's web. She seems to send me messages just when I most need them—a quick note, a quote on her website, or a Facebook post. Knowing Maureen wraps her arms around not only me, but also Drew and Anjuli, like our angel here on earth, reminds me how truly blessed I am.

Nothing is coincidence. Maureen and I were meant to meet. We were brought together by some unseen force. She had a gift to give, not once, but twice. She is here to remind me and to show me what my inner soul does not always remember: our loved ones are here with us, waiting on the other side for our reunion. We cannot waste what time we have here. We must reach out to others, and help them with what gifts we have to give. We must live life. Love life.

To me, Gail is "supermom." Even knowing what I know about grieving and the other side, I'm not sure I could get out of bed every day after physically losing my precious children. Everyone grieves in their own way, of course, but Gail has burrowed deep into the crevices of her soul and used her profound, life-shattering experience to help other grieving mothers.

During the summer of 2010, Gail, her husband, Jeremy, and Drew's fiancée, Jenna, came to see me for a reading. It was a gorgeous afternoon, just after the first anniversary of Drew's physical passing. Gail, in her usual unselfish way, had wanted so much for Jenna to experience a connection to Drew and so had asked for this meeting.

I came out of my office and greeted them all. Jenna was visibly nervous. I could feel her body tremble a bit as I hugged her. I took her clammy hand and led her into my office. Gail and Jeremy followed. Since Jenna was so nervous and this was her first reading experience, I was afraid it would be hard for Drew to make a clear connection. (The more relaxed a person is, the easier it is for spirit to come through.)

But before I could even explain to Jenna how the process works for me, Drew was chomping at the bit to come through. He spoke with magnificent clarity. I closed my eyes and began to share his message. Drew explained exactly what happened the day he drowned in the kayaking accident:

I wasn't even going to go. It was a last-minute decision. We [he and Jenna] had plans later that afternoon. I thought I could just squeeze a run in with the guys and be back in time for us to go out. You [Jenna] begged me not to go. I told you I would be fine. You said you couldn't live without me if something happened. I assured you I would be safe. My friends went down the river ahead of me. I came around a corner and got caught up on a rock. I really thought I could get out of it. I flipped and kept trying to fight against the rapids. I was really stuck. Anjuli was standing in front of me smiling. She took my hand and I knew everything would be okay.

Jenna sat with her mouth open and looked at Gail with shock and disbelief.

"Everything you just said is exactly what was said and what happened that day," Jenna shared. "I had a gut feeling something was going to happen to Drew. I begged him over and over again not to go."

I explained to Jenna that sometimes we get little glimpses into our "book of life," or what some Hindus and theosophists call the "akashic records." The akashic records are the universe's energetic imprints of a soul's journey: past, present, and future. Over the years I've met with many parents who secretly told me they had worried incredibly over the years about one of their children and had always had a gut feeling that something would happen to them. When I would hear this, I often thought that somewhere deep inside, on a soul level, these parents were tapping into a piece of the child's akashic record.

After my session with Gail and family, she sent me the most touching e-mail. I will always cherish it.

Dear Maureen,

Words can't express how much Jeremy and I appreciate your time, energy, and your gift. I hope you see and feel the wonder of the healing you nurture. Our time with you brought even more than we could ever have expected. Jenna needed to hear *everything* you [Drew and Anjuli] had to say. Jeremy is still glowing from the words you left him with and I am eternally grateful for what you brought to us.

You could not have been more accurate in your interpretation of what you "heard." You captured the essence of Drew, of Jeremy's mother, of the relationship between Jenna and Drew, of the bond between Anjuli and Drew, and Drew's need to reach out to Jenna to help her on her life's journey. I didn't want to say too much during the session, but you were so bang on that Jenna even asked me if I had spoken to you beforehand to let you know how things were going for her.

Please let me know if there is ever *anything* I can do for you, or for someone you're trying to help. I'm still searching for the venue to help others, so I'm open to anything that comes along. I believe in you and everything you are doing, and feel with all my being that you are meant to touch the lives of many. You have a gift and a message that will help people open their hearts to others and allow for great spiritual growth.

I hope *your child,* Drew, is okay. I still chuckle thinking of his comments the night you called me—how he wanted a brownie at 9:30 PM, and you told him it would give him diarrhea. Then you said, "I'm helping a mom who lost her son, and his name is Drew, too." And *he* said, "If he's dead, how does that help me?" Unknowingly, your son has your sense of humor already!

Thank you for your generous heart. Thank you for holding our precious children in your arms and delivering them to us one more time. Thank you for reminding us of their love and our eternal connection with them. You give the gift of yourself, and the gift of peace and hope and love. Maureen, you are truly an angel living among us, and we are blessed that our paths crossed.

Much love, always,

Gail and Jeremy

Birthdays, anniversaries, and holidays are the toughest time of year for anyone grieving, especially parents. This past Christmas, I was so overwhelmed by all of the young spirits around, I grabbed my chocolate lab, Ally, and decided to head to the river at the end of my street for an evening walk. I looked out the living room window to check the weather. Outside, snow lightly blanketed the neighborhood.

I took great efforts to cover every inch of my pasty-white, Irish skin. By the time I finished pulling on my thermal underwear, black Chili pants, green duck boots, Irish mohair sweater, seventies snorkel jacket—complete with furry hood—and an old wool scarf my grandmother crocheted years ago, I had lost three pounds from the effort and become light-headed from heat exhaustion!

There is something so serene about the first big snowfall. As I walked toward the river, I glanced over my shoulder to look at my footprints. Doing what I do, I fully expected to see many footprints, big and small, following me. I thought of the many children I connect with who have gone before their parents and siblings . . . the first to step onto the path to heaven. The children's words echo in my heart:

"Tell my parents I am okay. When I came over, everyone stood in a circle to greet me. I felt like I was wrapped in a warm blanket, and I knew everything would be all right. I was filled with love. There is no real time in heaven, and I take comfort in knowing I will see my parents and siblings again. I was the first to take the path, but I won't be the last. Tell them my love for them will never die. Tell them to smile and laugh for me—and not to feel guilty about it—because it fills my spirit with such joy to know they are living for me. I am living through them. I will make my presence known if they open their hearts to the many reminders I send them . . . a song on the radio, a coin with the date of my birth, a beautiful bird that catches their eye, my jersey number, a call with nobody on the other end, and, best of all, a dream where I hug or tell them, 'I'm not dead. I'm just *different*.'"

The holidays bring the joy of the season and the emptiness of missing a loved one. The children in spirit tell me, "I see my ornament! I see my tree!" Last year, one young boy in heaven told me exactly what his brother was getting from Santa. He also told me where Dad—that is, Santa—hid it.

For many of my families, this year will mark the first holidays they will spend without a special loved one. I want to assure you that this is a physical separation only, and you are not alone. Your children know how much you love and miss them. They want you to know they are happy and out of pain. The best gift you can give the loved one you miss is to believe in your heart that they are still a part of your life. Your thoughts speak directly to them. So, light the tree (even if it's a Charlie-Browner), hang the ornaments, light the menorah in their memory, light a candle in the window, and speak from your heart. Do all of this with the absolute knowing that you will be together again one day in the glory of heaven.

Walking back to my house from the river that night, I watched the white lights from the houses sparkling on the snow. Feeling the beautiful essence of the children, I stuck out my tongue and looked up to the sky, catching giant snowflakes on my tongue and giggling with delight. Dropping to the ground, I moved my arms and legs through the soft, light snow. It's the type of snow that would fail to make a good snowball or snowman, but it's just perfect for snow angels. I stopped to listen. Through the silence and stillness, I could hear the children laughing. They fill me with love and peace.

***

Can there be a more horrific pain to face than losing a child? Our children aren't supposed to leave this earthly world before us! Isn't that a rule somewhere? Well, it should be! Our children infuse our lives, soak through our pores, and warm our hearts. Beginning with their first tooth and their first step and through to their first school dance, sport event, recital, and graduation day—our lives are filled with the excitement of "what's next" when we become parents. From day one, we can't imagine life without them. How does one survive the unbearable loss of a child?

Everyone responds differently—respect that it's a personal pain. Give yourself permission to release your pain in whatever way you choose. You may not be able to return to your usual schedule, but find something that even for a brief second makes you feel alive again. Get outside and be a part of nature, let the sun reenergize you, walk along the beach. Look into a support group and bond with other parents going through the same journey. Find a grief counselor that you feel comfortable with.

We all need a reason for going on, a purpose for living. The children always tell me they want their parents to live for them and feel their presence close by. Our children's love and energy surround us daily. They send us messages through music, dreams, shooting stars, rainbows, cloud formations, heart-shaped rocks, animals, insects, birds, and other children. Finding your way to peace will be a daily struggle. Believe that your child is still a part of your life, holding you up with immeasurable strength, teaching you to trust you will all be together again one day.

7

Married to a Medium

What is it like being married to a medium? Well, I can't imagine it's easy. Just ask Greg, my husband. Our friends joke with him that he can't get away with anything because of my psychic abilities—and they are correct! At home, we are just like most of our friends and neighbors, trying to get through each day and raise our children right. On the off chance we have time to go out with friends, it can be a challenge. Greg is a private person, and he reminds me how important our rare family time is. Still, strangers approach me everywhere I go. I love to hear their stories of how I've helped them in some way, but Greg gets a bit frustrated. I understand his frustration because oftentimes, people will come up to me when we are out at a restaurant or even at the movies. They will say, "I know you're eating, but can I just ask you one question?"

Greg coaches many of our children's sports. He likes to share stories with me about how some of the kid's parents will ask him about me. Recently, while coaching basketball, the head coach asked, "Isn't your wife the one who talks to the dead? I've been to some of her shows." Greg was surprised to hear this from another guy. Luckily, the parents of most of my children's friends know what I do and are comfortable around me.

At the end of the last football season, I was at the field hanging out with other football moms. We had set up lawn chairs by the fence and were watching the kids practice. Greg was on the field coaching Drew, while my other son, Tyler, was practicing on the adjacent field. While we were laughing and sharing stories about our children, a wave of panic suddenly rushed through my body. I knew something had happened to Tyler. Just at that moment, Greg yelled to me to go see who was down on the other field. He saw a pile of kids on someone. I started running toward the field. One of the other moms yelled to me, "It's your son. He's hurt."

A fence separated me from getting to my son. As any good Spider-Woman-mother would do, I attempted to scale the fence (and got stuck at the top). One of the dads came running to the rescue and catapulted me over the fence. I ran to Tyler and got down on the ground with him, resting his head in my lap.

Greg came running over to see what was going on. I heard a loud voice in my head saying, "His leg is broken. Get him to the hospital now!" I relayed this information to Greg.

"His leg is broken. We need to call an ambulance."

"It's not broken. He's just overreacting," Greg quipped.

I glared at him and said, "Do you not remember what I do for a living? His leg *is* broken."

We rushed him to the hospital where it was confirmed his leg was broken in two places. He spent the next six months in a cast. When we got home, I politely reminded Greg I was right. "You should know that I pick up things going on with the family. If I insist I'm hearing the information, you should trust it," I said.

I was doing the dishes one Tuesday evening while Tyler and Drew were playing video games in the game room. I was gazing out the window at a cardinal who was peeking in and became so lost in thought that I didn't realize the water had turned pink.

"Ouch!" I yelled. I looked down to see a half-inch cut on my ring finger. Without realizing it, I had sliced my finger on a steak knife. As I quickly grabbed a piece of paper towel and wrapped it around the cut, I had a sudden vision of my cancer patient, Nick, who had just passed away.

Nick and I had become friends and kindred spirits during the months before he passed. He was in his late seventies when he was diagnosed with bladder cancer. I met with him weekly to give him healing treatments to reduce his pain and help him be more mobile.

Nick loved his wife and children beyond measure and loved to talk about them. I could sit and listen to Nick's stories for hours. We would laugh until we cried. He told me once he felt the love and warmth of the Blessed Mother Mary coming out of my hands. I shared with him my gift of communicating with spirits. Being a devout Catholic, he never said much about it. Near the end of his physical time here, he started to ask me questions about the afterlife and if anyone was trying to talk to him. I connected him with his mother and brothers in heaven. His mom died when he was only three years old. I think it gave him a lot of comfort to know she and his brothers were waiting for him.

Along with Nick's presence, another preternatural vision presented itself, like a movie playing in slow motion. I watched as I played ball with my boys in the yard. We then jumped in the car to go to my sister's house. In this movie, there was no dad. "Where's Greg?" I asked Nick.

"He passed away of a heart attack," the spirit stated matter-of-factly.

This was not a movie I wanted to star in. Life without Greg? And my children fatherless?

Wake me up from this nightmare now, I thought. *I must be imagining this. Anxiety is my middle name, after all. Greg is a thirty-five-year-old healthy man. He doesn't smoke and rarely drinks. There is no way he had or is about to have a heart attack..*

Just then I heard our SUV pull into the driveway and was snapped back into my present-day kitchen. I let out a sigh of relief. Dead men don't drive. I went upstairs to grab my boys' pajamas, and once there, I looked out the second-floor bedroom window at our driveway. Greg was slumped over the wheel of the SUV, his arms draped over the steering wheel and his face buried in the steering column. I ran down the stairs, skipping several steps, and almost landed flat on my ass. I couldn't get outside fast enough.

Running to the car, I shouted, "Greg, you're having a heart attack! Nick said you would!"

Greg slowly lifted his head and grimaced, "I'm just having some indigestion. I keep burping."

My relief was short-lived. As we walked into the house, Nick showed up again. This time he was even more insistent. *Greg is having a massive coronary. Call 911.*

I could hear the call now: Hi, my dead friend Nick said my husband is having a heart attack. Please make it snappy before he joins him.

Greg refused to let me call 911. After all, what would the neighbors think? He leaned on the kitchen counter. He was covered in sweat and turning pale gray. I watched him like a hawk. "I really think this is just indigestion," he insisted, clutching his chest and doubling over in pain. "It will pass if I let out a good belch." He still refused to let me call 911.

I quickly called my niece to come watch my two boys. "Stassia, it's me, Mo," I whispered. "Can you come over? I'm pretty sure Greg is having a heart attack and he won't let me call an ambulance. Hurry."

Stassia arrived in no time, and I already had helped Greg to the car.

Once in the emergency-room triage at our local hospital, we both spoke at once when asked what the problem was. He said, "Bad indigestion," and I said, "I think he's having a heart attack."

The triage nurse did the usual tests—blood pressure, temperature, EKG, blood work, and so on. After waiting about an hour, an alleged doctor entered the room. He looked like Doogie Howser on uppers. As he spoke, his eyes darted around the room, looking up at the ceiling, down at the floor—anywhere but directly at us. His tone was condescending and cold.

"Mr. Hancock, all your tests came back normal. You're thirty-five years old, you don't smoke, you don't have high blood pressure, you're active. You are *not* having a heart attack. You have acid reflux."

I jumped in with my two-cents worth. "You mean to tell me that a cold sweat, grayish complexion, shortness of breath, and a death clutch on the chest has no resemblance to heart-attack symptoms?"

Doogie did not like my line of questioning. He finally looked right at me, "Mrs. Hancock, esophageal spasms mimic the signs of a heart attack. Your husband is having a bad case of acid reflux. He's young, healthy, and doesn't smoke. He is definitely not having a heart attack. You can both go home now."

Greg looked over at me with a smirk on his face. He leaned over and whispered in my ear, "See, I told you it was just indigestion."

With trepidation, I put my jacket on and started the long walk down the hospital corridor with my gray-faced husband by my side. Something still didn't feel right. Nick didn't show up in my kitchen for a bad case of indigestion.

Suddenly, a loud voice caught my attention. I turned around. A male nurse was jogging toward us. He was red-faced and wide-eyed. When I think back on this, I wonder if he was an earth angel.

"Mr. Hancock, you have to come back to the emergency room. You did have a heart attack! I took a look at your last blood test, and it indicates you've had some kind of damage to your heart."

In complete silence, with our heads hung low, we walked back to the examining room in emergency.

Dr. Doogie sauntered nonchalantly into the room, rubbing Mr. Sandman's dust from his eyes. I could feel my Irish blood rise.

"I was waiting for Greg's last blood test to come back," he said, "and sure enough, he did in fact have a heart attack."

As my forked tongue began to slither out to dope-slap Doogie, my mother's voice echoed in my head: "If you don't have anything nice to say, don't say anything at all." I took the high road (my dad's saying) and channeled my inner Irish into action. I'd already made up my mind hours ago when I knew Greg had had a heart attack—he would *not* stay at this local hospital with a bunch of Doogies playing Operation!

A man walked in the room who resembled Dr. McDreamy on *Grey's Anatomy*. I fully expected him to say, "I'm not a doctor, but I play one on TV." With his perfectly coifed hair and brilliant white smile, he reached out his hand to introduce himself. "I'm Dr. Carlson, head of cardiology."

Laying a hand on Greg's shoulder and looking intently in his eyes, he said, "We need to get you to Boston immediately. You have a thrombosis (a blood clot), and it's moving toward your heart. If you had walked out that door, you would have died in your sleep."

Greg was transferred to Brigham and Women's Hospital where he received an immediate angioplasty procedure. A stent was placed to open a 90-percent blockage to the main artery in the left side of his heart. The procedure went well, and I was permitted to see Greg in recovery a few hours after the surgery. As I walked down the long corridor, I could hear a lot of yelling coming from the recovery room. When I got to the double doors, my heart sank as I saw ten to twelve hospital employees gathered around Greg! *Oh no*, I thought, *he must have had another attack!* They were all jumping up and down, high-fiving one another and clapping. *Wow, they must really be proud of themselves for jump-starting my husband's heart*, I imagined. I literally had to squeeze my way through the mosh pit to get to the bed. There was no defibrillator nearby, no syringes on the bed, no leftover equipment . . . just the TV playing and the Red Sox winning their first World Series since 1918.

Has there ever been a time in your life that you knew something was true—I mean, you just *knew* it, even if you didn't know how you knew it. People may have tried to tell you that you were wrong, but something inside you wouldn't let go of the truth. Trust that feeling. Be like a dog with a bone and don't let go. What's the worst thing that could happen if you followed through on your intuition despite everyone's objections? You might feel like a fool for a few moments, but I bet you'd still be glad you listened to yourself.

What is your inner wisdom telling you right now? You know what I mean: that nagging feeling that must pay attention regarding some part of your life. It can feel like an inner knowing, like a gut-wrenching "no," or like a part of your body is trying to get your attention. That nagging feeling won't go away if it has something important to tell you. Pay attention. It's better to look like a fool (take it from one who knows) and follow through on your feeling rather than ignore it and regret it later. Be an advocate for yourself and others. Don't put things off or wait for something to work itself out on its own. Take action, take charge, and take care.

Slow down for a few moments. Sit quietly and ask, "What does my inner wisdom want me to know right now?"

8

Transitions

I spent most of my childhood fearing death because I had been so ill for so long. And because of my long hospital stay, I also had severe separation anxiety. Anytime my parents or siblings left the house, I thought for sure they would never return, that they would be swept into a dark abyss, carried away by the grim reaper. My mind had a field day with all the possible (and even impossible) scenarios ending in death. Then, oddly enough, my fear of death was lifted in the most unlikely of ways.

I was eight years old when my mother and I found my great-aunt Libby dead on the floor of her one-bedroom apartment not too far from our house. A feisty single woman ahead of her time, Libby had worked her way up to an executive position at the telephone company.

My mother checked in on her several times a week, and she dragged my siblings and me along to help "clean up" as mom prepared meals, washed clothing, and sipped tea with Libby.

Hundreds of hairpins covered Libby's living room floor. She should have been declared legally blind—in fact, she typically answered the *closet* door when the front doorbell rang. Even though I made a face every time she hugged me—she squeezed me until I couldn't breathe—I secretly longed for her tight hugs . . . and the Fig Newtons she "baked from scratch." (I now realize that she didn't actually bake them "for hours" before our arrival.)

On a hot, humid morning in June, my mother asked me to go with her to Aunt Libby's. After we rang the buzzer in the foyer of the apartment building, it usually took Libby a few minutes to shuffle to the intercom. This time, after about five minutes had passed, I sensed my mother's anxiety.

"Why won't she answer the door?" I asked. Do you think she's looking for us in the closet?"

My mother walked outside and tried to peek in the window of Libby's basement apartment. I saw her eyes widen and her face turn pale.

"What's wrong? Can you see Aunt Libby? Is she okay?" I asked.

Frantically, my mother rang the buzzer to Libby's neighbor, Joe, a maintenance man in his sixties.

"We need to get in Libby's apartment immediately!" my mother demanded.

Without a word, Joe unlocked the door and my mother rushed in. Libby, dressed in her purple-flowered housecoat, lay on her side next to her recliner. My mother tried to get me to stay out in the hall, but I was frozen in the doorway, staring down at Aunt Libby's lifeless body. Her face was grayish-purple and her hair was wild and frizzy. (She usually kept her hair in a neat bun, held together by 250 bobby pins!)

"Is she dead?" I whispered.

My mother nodded.

I could sense that my aunt was no longer in the shell lying in front of me. I felt a light breeze gently flow across my face and my nostrils filled with the scent of her perfume. My fears melted away with the realization that I could still feel Aunt Libby and sense her hugs. All that she was and meant to me was not gone. I grinned from ear to ear as I carried this peaceful feeling in my heart all the way home. My fear of death was lifted. The lasting gift left behind by Aunt Libby was a godsend for me. My mother looked at me through the rearview mirror and asked, "Are you okay? Why are you smiling?"

I responded, "I'm fine and so is Auntie Libby. Mom, she's right here with us."

Death came and went throughout the years—grandparents, aunts, uncles, neighbors, and beloved pets. (I must give honorable mention to my hamster, Sunshine, who died of an apparent heart attack. I held him in the palm of my hand—performing CPR with my pinky in a desperate attempt to save his furry little life. Even then I knew he needed to leave behind his leased vehicle and continue driving that hamster wheel in heaven.) I started to accept that when it was someone's time, they had to go. I still missed them terribly, but the fears I used to have about death diminished significantly.

Today I dedicate much of my time to helping people understand death and dying. Over the years, I've created a unique spiritual hospice that assists thousands of families through the "death" process and guides them through this beautiful transition. I am completely humbled as I hold the light high for families who feel alone in the dark.

I helped one such family at Children's Hospital in Boston when their newborn was being taken off life support. Olivia had been born with a congenital heart defect and had been immediately placed on the heart transplant list. Two weeks after her birth, I walked into the hospital's neonatal intensive care unit (NICU). Around me, machines beeped, ventilators hissed, and tubes made suction noises. These sounds brought me back in time to when I was the one lying in a crib, fighting for my life with lead-paint poisoning.

Olivia's tiny fingers were wrapped around her mom, Julie's, pinky. Pete, Olivia's dad, leaned over the crib, stroking her face. Tears ran down Pete's face onto the soft, pink bunny blanket under Olivia.

"Olivia is talking to me," I gently told her parents. (While I had long communicated with the dead, talking to the living—to a conscious mind—was still new to me. I had once helped the family of a six-year-old nonverbal boy communicate with him without words. During a visit, he told me (mind to mind) that he had gone horseback riding in Freetown, a small rural town in Massachusetts. When I relayed this to his parents, they were flabbergasted. Dylan had indeed taken his first horseback riding lesson in Freetown that afternoon.)

Now, Olivia was reaching out to me.

"What is she saying?" Julie quietly asked.

"She said you were singing 'Somewhere Over the Rainbow' last night when you got home."

Julie's mouth dropped open as her eyes filled up. "Yes," she said. "I rocked my three-year-old, Cameron, to sleep singing that song. I told him that his sister was going to heaven tomorrow, and we needed to pray for her."

"Can you tell Olivia that we love her and we'll miss her?" Pete asked.

"Pete, you can tell her that yourself," I answered. "She hears you. She can feel your love. You don't need me to translate that."

Just then, a doctor pulled back the curtain and poked her head in. "We are going to take Olivia off the heart machine within the hour." Olivia's condition quickly deteriorated and she was one of many babies waiting for a new heart. Time simply ran out for Olivia

Julie and Pete kissed Olivia on her head, face, hands, and feet. They took turns kissing her beautiful heart-shaped lips.

We gathered in a tight circle and held hands. Julie whispered to me that Pete didn't believe in an afterlife and wasn't sure there was a God. I secretly asked Olivia to help me find the right words to ease her family through this transition. When I started to speak, it felt like someone else took over:

"Olivia will soon leave her struggling heart and body behind. Even though I can't fully explain why her physical time here was so short, she will always be connected to you both.

"We come into this world with a soul contract that determines how long we will be here and what we will accomplish. We teach one another lessons, and often it takes time to digest and embrace the meaning of those lessons. The meaning of Olivia's lessons and gifts to you will become clear over time. But her presence will be felt in undeniable ways. She has touched many lives already and will continue to do so."

I took Pete aside and told him his deceased grandparents were in the room, along with Julie's dad. Her dad said to tell Pete that the Canadians were here to welcome Olivia to the other side.

"I keep hearing two strange 'E' names—like Esmeralda and Eugenia," I said.

"Oh my God, my grandmother's name is Esdelle and my grandfather is Eugene!" exclaimed Pete.

"There's also a yellow lab by your feet, Pete," I laughed.

"Jeeter!" Pete yelled out looking around his legs. "That's our yellow lab who was hit by a car a few months ago."

The team of cardiologists then entered the room. They looked at Julie, and she nodded. They took a few minutes to remove the many tubes attached to Olivia's tiny body. A doctor handed Olivia to Julie as she sat in the rocking chair.

"I promised Olivia I would nurse her before she goes to heaven. I want her to have a part of me with her," said Julie, as tears poured down her cheeks. She soaked a small swab with breast milk and gently placed it in Olivia's mouth and around her lips.

I quickly left the room to wait behind the curtain. I heard Julie singing "Somewhere Over the Rainbow" through her tears.

Pete said, over and over, "That's my girl. That's daddy's little girl."

Pete and Julie both held Olivia during her final moments. Afterward,

Julie would tell me how good it felt to hold Olivia without any tubes or beeping noises.

It took about fifteen minutes for Olivia to take her last breath. Julie said she felt such peace in the room, and Olivia looked angelic. Something by the window caught their attention. They were stunned to see a rainbow peeking out of the clouds.

Before I left the NICU floor, Julie ran up and hugged me. She whispered in my ear, "What you told Pete in there about his grandparents and my dad made him believe there *is* a God. Thank you."

I used to wonder why *I* had to be the messenger for the God squad. I often feel like one of Charlie's Angels, waiting to see the man talking on the outside line. Sometimes, when I drive up to a home with someone inside who is about to pass, I freeze before I get out, praying for guidance. At times, my thoughts wander and my own fears take over. Often I think to myself, *What in the world am I going to say to them? How do I look a mother in the eye and tell her not to be afraid, her kids will be just fine, as three young children call out, "Is my mom going to be okay? Will she get better?"*

And then there are the many questions and fears people share with me when they are close to passing over: *What happens when we die? Where do we go? What do we do? Is there complete darkness? I'm afraid I won't see my children. I'm afraid I'm letting them down. I'm scared of the unknown.*

Some of these questions will be fully answered when I get there myself. For now, I trust what I've been told by spirit and what I have witnessed firsthand in the presence of those leaving their body.

So, what does happen to the soul at the time of a physical passing? In most instances, I believe the soul leaves the body at the moment of death. In working with clients in a comatose state, I've noticed something a little different. It's as if part of the soul has journeyed on and the other part struggles to hang on here—not quite ready to leave.

My older sister Marygrace, who remained in a coma for almost a year after being hit by a car in 1980, helped me understand what it was like for her during that time. She talked about seeing a stunning white light and being so drawn to it (much like many accounts of near-death experiences). Beyond the light she could see some of our relatives in spirit. Talking to Jesus and Mary, she expressed, was her greatest joy while visiting the other side. She said she could hear us talking to her in the hospital room and struggled to answer. Her experience sounded similar to dreams in which you are trying to yell and no sound comes out, and it takes all your strength to wake from the dream to find your voice.

Jesus told Marygrace it wasn't her time and she needed to go back. She revealed to me that the experience on the other side was so breathtaking she felt torn about coming back.

"I felt much love over there. Everyone seemed so happy. It was a lot like here, with trees, flowers, and houses. I wasn't afraid and felt like I was home again," she recalled.

When my sister came out of the coma in late summer of 1981, I noticed some remarkable things. She mouthed the words to songs on the radio. Yeah, on the surface this doesn't seem overly interesting. However, these songs had been released *after* she slipped into a coma!

Apparently, a part of her remained present in that hospital bed, even though she seemed to be in a deep slumber.

Another mind-blowing revelation Marygrace shared with us was that she knew her precious dog, Heidi, had passed away a few months before she came out of the coma. When asked how she knew, she responded, "I heard you all talking about it."

You may wonder how the thoughts and feelings of family members affect the dying. We can't help but want to do everything in our power to assist a loved one who is suffering. What I've noticed is that most family members feel helpless and are not sure how to handle what's going on around them. It's important to try to let go of fear and stay positive, even under grave circumstances. Energy is a powerful tool, and the thoughts and feelings we give off—positive and negative— surround our loved ones.

Oftentimes, when someone is about to pass, the dying will hang on until everyone is able to come and say good-bye. On other occasions, spirit has told me, the dying *couldn't* pass while the room was full—it was too hard to say good-bye, and emotions were too overwhelming for a peaceful transition. In such cases, the dying person waits until everyone goes home, then passes quietly, in private.

Having been present during many "last breath" ceremonies, here is what I have personally experienced and observed. Not long before the body retires, I've seen the dying get that one last gust of wind. Strangely, they suddenly seem very alert—almost as if they are rallying one last time to share memories, laughter, last wishes, and, sometimes, a good meal.

Those on the other side "line up" as they wait, and sometimes they bombard me with messages for the loved one about to join them. The room is electrified with the presence of unconditional love from both sides. The dying one's breath slows down and becomes shallow, like that of a newborn baby. When I lay my hands on the physical body, my arms tingle as I try to catch my own breath, overcome with the energy surging through me. I believe this surge of energy is the body's way of preparing to separate from its spirit.

I often cry tears of joy as I feel the soul shift in its transition . . . just as water transitions from a liquid to a solid, then dissolves and recycles back to liquid . . . the soul is pure and boundless . . . eternal.

When a client is about to cross over, close family members from the other side are present in the room. They usually start to pop in and out about a week or two before the passing. Within a couple of days of the transition, they are present day and night. I hear them clearly, and, most times, I can see them standing beside the person with a hand on their shoulder. I share their profound messages of hope and peace with the living family members gathered around, providing the most unique family reunion ever.

Being witness to such intimate happenings is humbling, breathtaking, gut-wrenching, and heartfelt. I am in constant awe at the strength of every man, woman, and child who travels on the road to transition, leaving behind the shell of who they were to us and embracing the beauty of their true spirit self—the essence of who they are. I especially remember one beautiful crossing over I witnessed. . . .

Mary, a woman in her late sixties, was about to pass. Her three daughters gathered around her. I massaged her feet to help her relax.

I moved up to whisper in her ear, "Your husband is here, Mary. He's holding your hand, smiling, and says he can't wait to dance with you again."

With her eyes closed, she smiled.

I looked up at her daughter, Erin. "Who is William?" I asked.

"Oh my, that's my father's name!" she exclaimed in delight.

"I'm also hearing a woman loudly saying, 'Tell her Margaret is here too.'"

Mary's other daughter, Katie, giggled, "Her mother is Margaret!"

I continued talking to Mary. "Everyone is waiting for you. Your brother is here, his wife, and your friend Betty. I also see a German shepherd pacing back and forth."

All three girls shouted at once, "Buddy!"

Mary pulled on my hand. I leaned down to hear her. "Will my girls be okay? I wish I could see Erin get married next month."

"The girls will be more than okay. You will be at the wedding, and Erin will feel your presence. You will guide and support them in a different way now. This beautiful bond you have with your girls will continue through eternity."

What happened next will be forever imbedded in my treasure chest of memories. Erin hopped into the bed and began stroking her mother's hair; her sister Christina, lay on the other side of the bed. Katie was sitting in the chair by the window. Mary sat straight up and extended her arms out. The sparkle in her eyes returned as her face lit up. The room filled with the scent of fresh roses. She looked right past us as she let out a knowing sigh. As she leaned back against the pillows, she closed her eyes and whispered, "Bill, you're really here."

Her breathing stopped. Time stood still for the next few moments. We hugged one another as tears of joy fell freely and gently celebrated Mary's departure from her fragile, physical shell. She had left all her pain behind.

"Where do they go after they pass? Do they hang around for a while?" Many people ask me these types of questions. We all want to know the answers. In my readings, spirits often tell me that they were present for their services, and I hear specific details about what was put in the coffin, surprise visitors they never cared for, what was said in their eulogy, and who said it, along with many other detailed bits of information that prove to me they actually take pride in these services. I recently connected with a woman in spirit who told her daughter that the undertaker did a horrible job on her hair. She laughed and said she secretly tried to fix it when nobody was around.

People who pass in sudden and tragic ways (especially teens and young adults), sometimes go through more of an adjustment period as they transition. I've heard other mediums speak of spirits being "stuck" between two worlds. My view is a bit different. I feel that the transition can take longer when the passing is unexpected. Eventually, the spirit body is guided and soothed by loved ones who have passed before them. The thoughts and feelings of those left behind, such as a parent of a young child, are instrumental in helping the child move forward in its new spirit body.

Parents I meet with who have had children pass often say they fear they are keeping their child here in the physical world and not allowing them to leave peacefully because of their own pain and grief. They are afraid the child will no longer be connected to them if they let them go. I assure them that the spiritual loving bond they have together can never be broken by this temporary physical separation. And without *some* preparation time, such as in the case of the terminally ill, these spirits might stick around longer as they work to adjust to and realize what has happened to them.

By letting our loved ones go physically, we actually help speed up the transformation from the physical body to the "light body" or spirit body. This way, spirit is in a better position to communicate more quickly with those left behind through sending them signs and visiting them in dreams.

"What are our loved ones in spirit doing on the other side? Do they have jobs? Do they know what's going on for us here?" These are other questions I'm often asked.

The life review comes soon after the initial shift to spirit. I'm told we are shown the Book of Life. It reveals all the good things we did in this life and areas in which we could have done better. It lists the challenges we agreed to go through and how we handled them. At some point, and I'm sure it's different for each spirit, we are given our assignment on the other side. My interpretation of this is that we are given a job to do, and it usually involves helping others. Many young people in spirit report to me that they are now working with children on the other side—as counselors, teachers, and guides—as well as guiding loved ones on the earthly plane.

Loved ones in spirit return to the physical realm in full force to offer
guidance, support, strength, and love during especially trying times.
When someone here is ill or struggling, the prayers and thoughts we
send to loved ones in spirit are received immediately. Spirit can't always
"fix" the problem or heal the sickness, but they can make their presence known and help us here to know they are aware of what's going
on. They also come forward during times of celebration—a birthday,
anniversary, special holidays, weddings, graduations, and so on.

What I've noticed soon after someone's passing are the signs that
pop up everywhere signaling us that they are still around. Sometimes
we miss the little signs the spirit sends as we look for the big ones or
for a specific sign. But it is when we are not looking that we receive
our heart's desire. How often have you been zoning out while driving
and suddenly the words to a song on the radio get your attention? The
words speak to you as if they are coming directly from the person you
miss most in spirit.

If you learn to quiet your mind and put aside the constant chatter
and worry, you become more receptive to the ways your loved ones in
spirit try to get your attention.

There is no time as we know it on the other side, and all who go
home before us know this. And they are content knowing we will be
along when we are supposed to, according to our own soul contracts.

One of the most provocative questions I'm often asked is, "Do we
reincarnate?"

Being raised in a strict Catholic family, I was told there was no such
thing as reincarnation. But I had been fascinated with the idea of rein-

carnation from childhood on and had read several books about it.

The big debate regarding reincarnation has many facets. If we do come back repeatedly, which I firmly believe, how long does it take us to return? Is it our choice to come back or not? Why would we come back? Are there more lessons to learn for our souls to evolve? And just what constitutes an evolved soul?

Quantum physics teaches us that we are all made up of energy and vibrations. Scientists are finally embracing what mystics and avatars have been teaching for thousands of years: energy cannot die. For me, this explains in a scientific way why we still exist after we shed our physical shells.

In choosing to come back to the physical (I do feel it is an individual choice, although I'm convinced *I* was pushed), we return to work through challenges we agreed to go through for our soul's learning and growth. Coming into each physical lifetime, we have a set of goals to help us reach our highest vibrational level (some call it "enlightenment"). The most basic challenges and lessons we must face and learn involve loving unconditionally; letting go of unwanted anger, guilt, and hatred; being nonjudgmental; acting kindly toward all; volunteering and sharing; being honest; and working through fears.

A great example of the existence of a past life comes directly from my own child. At three years old, my son Tyler sat at the kitchen table drawing. I looked at the paper and saw several Chinese symbols.

"Tyler, what are you writing?" I asked.

"My Chinese stuff," he said confidently. "I lived in a building with no windows with lots of other kids. My parents died, and they put me in this place with no toys."

I decided this must have been an orphanage. Tyler then started to talk in what seemed like Chinese! I took the paper to a friend who grew up in China. She said the writings were, in fact, Chinese. There were random words like "boy," "airplane," and "dog."

Because of my work and all the profound, loving messages I've received from the other side, I no longer fear death. Don't get me wrong. I don't want anyone close to me to physically depart, but I have complete confidence that we will all be together again in what seems like a blink of the eye to those waiting for us to "come home." We miss our loved ones in spirit, but they don't miss us. They have a knowing beyond our comprehension that we will all be okay, and we will all be reunited with one another.

How we view death affects how we live our lives. Have you ever stopped to really examine your beliefs about death to see if they are still true for you? If we are afraid of death, that fear will influence every part of our lives, causing us to cling to the familiar, to fear loss. Fearing death prevents us from living life with full gusto each and every day. It also keeps us from feeling a deep sense of joy and freedom.

While it's true that each of us will transition to spirit one day, what is it that really "dies"? Not our spirit; our spirit is eternal. What dies is simply the body, the vehicle that housed our spirit. One might say that death is simply the shift into being purely nonphysical form once again. Like the caterpillar that emerges as a unique and beautiful butterfly, our loved ones leave the casing of the body and return to their full spiritual essence.

Take a moment to imagine what it might be like in spirit. Feel the vibration of pure love, joy, and boundlessness. Breathe it in. Your own spirit is connected to that place. You might experience a deeper sense of peace within you as you do this exercise. You might also feel the presence of a loved one in spirit right there with you. Enjoy . . . breathe . . . trust. All is well.

9

Mission for the Missing

I pulled out my old work boots from my high-school days working the farm at the agricultural school. Today I'm working my first missing-person case. I've avoided delving into the area of missing and murdered persons over the years—I was always fearful that I'd be putting my family in danger. Knowing I could use my abilities to bring closure to so many families, however, allowed me to put aside my fears.

As we crossed the border from Massachusetts to Vermont, my palms began to sweat, my heart rate increased, and my legs twitched. My body was reacting to the surge of powerful energy coursing through it. In an almost dreamlike state, I felt I was facing a choice between fight or flight, and my wayward body was trying to do both.

I glanced over at the private detective, Alan, in the driver's seat, hoping he had some inkling that I was having a panic attack. I had heard from other investigators that he was also an EMT. If I passed out, he'd know what to do. Alan, a tall, compassionate man in his early fifties, squeezed the wheel of the truck harder, gazing straight ahead. His associate, Rod, in the backseat, leaned forward to point a small handheld video camera at me.

"She says we're a half hour from the spot she disappeared," I told the men.

As we drove through the winding roads and back woods of this mountainous territory, my mind raced with thoughts of the kidnapping and murder of Laura, a college student.

I heard a loud, high-pitched buzzing in my ear and knew immediately that Laura wanted to communicate something. There were flashes of darkness and icy roads and headlights blinding my vision, and finally, the impact filled my head and mind's eye. I saw a dark midsize car turn a corner and hit a tree. A young woman's head hit the windshield. My head throbbed and I felt disoriented.

As we got close to the area of the disappearance, my feet and legs tingled.

"She says we're five minutes away," I let the men know again.

I was petrified. *What the hell was I thinking? I've never done a missing-person search. Who do I think I am, Allison DuBois from* Medium? My left leg went completely numb as we turned a sharp corner. I could feel stomach acid burning my throat.

"Pull over! I'm going to throw up."

Alan locked up his brakes as he pulled over to the side of the road. I jumped out, ran behind a tree, and vomited violently.

"I have to tell you something," Alan said. "The tree you're standing next to is the one Laura crashed into on the night of her disappearance."

I felt energy brewing in the spot where I stood. The leaves on the trees were completely still, yet a gust of wind brushed against my face and lifted my hair. A shiver traveled through my body. Suddenly, I felt compelled to walk farther along the street. With each step, my breathing slowed and echoed in my head. A murky film covered my eyes. The trees were no longer visible. I felt like I was moving in slow motion, almost in a trance. My body was no longer my own. In front of me I saw a tunnel. Before my mind could process the scene, I felt my feet quickly moving beneath me. Jogging at a fast pace, frantically looking over my shoulder, I felt fear rush through my body and send shock waves down my spine. I trembled uncontrollably when I reached the end of the tunnel. Like a search dog following the scent of a subject, I reached the end of the trail. Drawn toward the house on the corner that sat on a hill, I stood at the edge of the property, staring at the porch.

I felt like Laura was trying to tell me something about this house. Suddenly, the door to the porch swung open. A stalky man in his mid- to late forties stepped out. Our eyes locked and the hair on the back of my neck stood up. Could this man be responsible for Laura's disappearance? My connection with Laura's energy seemed to fade.

I could see the detective's truck out of the corner of my eye as I shuffled backward toward the back of the SUV. Alan reached out his arm and pulled me into the truck. He quickly sped away.

"Maureen, sorry to leave you hanging like that, but we wanted to see what you could pick up from him. He's our main suspect. All of the neighbors are afraid of him and his ex-wife alluded to the fact that he may have killed his former girlfriend many years ago."

"Laura kept showing me a small white house. It looked almost like a long mobile home. I think she was trying to tell me the suspect lived in the white shit hole."

I rolled down the window and inhaled the clean mountain air. I felt my energy wane, and became dizzy.

"Maureen, you look so pale," said Rod.

"Are you okay to continue?" asked Alan.

"Maybe we can grab a quick sandwich." I knew food would help me refuel.

We stopped at a small log cabin, the only sandwich shop in town— also home to the only gas station, barbershop, volunteer firefighters, hardware store, and general merchandise business in town. It strangely resembled Oleson's Mercantile from *Little House on the Prairie*.

When we finished lunch, I told Rod and Alan that Laura wanted me to drive back toward the red barn, specifically to the sixth street past the mercantile.

"Take a right at this dirt road. She says to stop halfway up the hill. Pull over."

I leaped out of the car and climbed a small dirt hill into the woods. My work boots disappeared into the soft, claylike sand. I could see the red barn to the right, and Laura pointed to an area about five hundred feet past the barn.

"Have you searched this area behind the barn?"

"No, we searched around the suspect's house and up near the tennis courts at the top of the hill. We can get a team of search dogs in here for the Fourth of July weekend."

Private Investigator Alan Tate's account of the holiday weekend search:

Why do I feel anxious? We've been working on this investigation for about a year and a half. We've been searching with cadaver dogs for days. Why do I feel nervous now about what we'll find out?

Having been an investigator for over twenty-five years, I'm a pretty black-and-white kind of guy. I believe in the facts and the truth—find the facts and truth, and a case hopefully comes to a positive end.

This is different. Neither my peers nor I had ever worked with a medium. Having seen Maureen at an investigators' luncheon and seeing what she did to a former police officer, a former U. S. Navy Seal, and an FBI agent got my attention.

She brought through facts that nobody except the person and close family members could have known. She had the former Navy Seal sweating through his shirt and the FBI agent in tears. What was this and how could we use this to assist us in finding these kids?

I will never forget the trip to Vermont with Maureen. She described the person of interest with such detail, adding facts that were not yet known to investigators. She pointed out an area about three football fields in length in the woods near the suspect's house.

Three weeks later, we returned with the K–9 teams, support personnel, and investigators. It was July and the weather was sunny and hot. Everyone met and we had our morning briefing. The area was described and the goal like always was to determine if there were human remains' scent.

The mapping was done, segments assigned, and the teams took to the woods. Working through the morning the teams came up blank.

Each segment is done twice. One dog will work it, we let the segment sit for a bit, and then another dog will work it. Like pitchers, even dogs have an off day. We need to make sure every segment is worked to the best of each team's abilities.

We make sure to provide plenty of rehab time for the dogs and handlers, as well as videographers and support people. Every team has a video person assigned to it and we record all searches in this way.

That day, lunch was way too quick—sandwiches, lots of water and sports drinks, a few high-protein snacks, and back into the woods.

About an hour into the second half of the day, we got word one of the teams' K-9 had had an indication for human remains' scent.

Just a quick word about these teams. The dogs go through years of training and never stop training. The teams travel the country, so we use the most experienced trainers as well as local training through various volunteer groups, many times in association with police officers or troopers who are trainers for their departments.

Each team has a résumé that lists every training class, exercise, and search they have participated in. The dogs are specifically trained to detect human remains' scent and some of the dogs are further trained to be used in water to detect the scent. These dogs differ from those that follow scent from an article of clothing—the tracking dogs, and those that pick up any live human scent—the air-scent dogs.

As is protocol, we pulled the team that had indication of scent out of the woods and prepared another team to verify. No markings are left at the site to give a visual cue but the handler knows where he or she is going.

The second team hit the woods. It took a few minutes to get into the area, and the other teams were now out of the woods and on the road standing by if needed.

Word came over the radio, "We have a positive indication." We pull the second team out and I discuss our next step. The team from Connecticut, which we've used on many searches, has a dog that works forensic cases.

She has a documented find on a piece of bone about 750 years old while on an archaeological dig in Louisiana. It's believed the bone belonged to persons who traveled from South America to the southern part of the United States by boat.

The dog is also on the National Center for Missing and Exploited Children's call-out list and has documented finds in her home state. She's a Portuguese water dog and works somewhat differently than many cadaver dogs.

The handler and dog went into the woods. I followed behind about twenty feet. From the dog's body language we knew she had picked up on something. She went to the same area the first two dogs were at and gave us an indication. She didn't stop there. In ever widening circles she worked the area outward from the indication, attempting to see if she could find a source other than where she was. Further and further out and then, without any additional indication, she went back to the spot and again gave her handler the indication. This dog, known as *the closer* due to her skills, is telling her handler, "There is human remains' scent here, I've checked the surrounding area, and this is the place, nowhere else."

We moved the team back and looked at the ground. No mounds, no depressions. Nothing that we could visually determine that had been disturbed.

The metal detectors were brought in and five investigators worked out from the spot in different directions. They found a few beer cans, an old wiper blade, and barbed wire but nothing that raised suspicion.

The area's GPS coordinates were taken. It was photographed and videotaped. We continued with the rest of the segments without any positive results.

Three dogs, one of which is one of the best in the country, all had identified an indication of human remains at the scene. No doubt it was there, but was it Laura's or somebody else's? Could we have found where she was at one point?

One theory is as follows: Laura went missing in early March. This part of the country is very cold all winter and the ground is frozen solid. Even the funeral homes do not perform burials until midspring. If Laura was killed and stored, could this be where she spent the winter only to be moved once spring came?

Rod put all the video of Maureen onto CDs. We sent the CDs, our report of the day's search, and our results to the Vermont State Police Major Crimes Unit.

We know from speaking with the locals that the State Police came into the area with their forensic team and performed a dig of the site. What they did or didn't find we don't know. In most of these cases information flows one way, from the volunteer investigators, like us, and K-9 teams to the police department handling the case.

Had Maureen found Laura's holding place? We believe so, not because we want to but because in her hours in this small northern New England town she gave the investigators information that in some cases took them over a year to find! Apparently, there is more to the black-and-white scenario we work with and more than just the facts we can see and prove. Most of us have never ventured into the area of spirit communicating with us from the other side.

A few weeks after the search, I received a phone call from Rod. The state police had reviewed the tapes and had interviewed him for almost two hours as to their authenticity. They wanted to confirm that what they saw on the CDs about Maureen's actions and words happened as they were portrayed. Rod told them yes, that was what happened.

The one line that sticks with me is what one of the troopers asked of him. "Who is this Maureen Hancock?"

Looking back, I am happy with my decision to put my fears aside and start using my ability to help in missing-person cases. Word quickly spread through law enforcement and the private investigation community about the progress we made on this case. Currently, I am working on several cases across the United States. I have assisted in bringing home several living children and adults who have recently gone missing. I do all of this work on a pro bono basis and have joined forces with Alan Tate to form a nonprofit charity called "Mission for the Missing." The foundation will provide services, equipment and support to families facing the unthinkable—a missing loved one.

We are all intuitive beings. Some have a higher vibration or ability to tap into this innate gift. Others need a gentle nudge or wake-up call. Our minds are always racing and trying to explain the unexplainable. We are constantly in a hurry. I always say, "Take your time and hurry up." When you take a few minutes out of your busy day to breathe and be aware of where you store your stress, together we can peel away the layers of your tension to reveal your heart.

Have you ever thought of someone only to have them call minutes later? Or a voice echoes in your mind to look to your left just as a tractor-trailer almost creams you. Is that a coincidence or are we being protected and guided from beyond? Trust is a big part of tuning in, along with learning to quiet the mind chatter so our senses and intuition have a clear channel to tap into.

The following exercise is the first step in clearing the channel:

Find a quiet place to sit or lay down. Turn off your cell phone, television, and any other distractions. Start by taking some deep, cleansing belly breaths. Breathe in through your nose, hold it for a count of two, and exhale. Let go of the day's stresses and allow your mind to focus on your breath. Taking a full diaphragm breath (from your belly) brings much-needed oxygen to all the cells and muscles in your body. Most of us get only half of the oxygen we need, thereby causing tension in our neck and upper back. Imagine your lower belly as a balloon inflating on the inhale and deflating on the exhale. Count your breath. This will help when interrupting thoughts creep in. Don't fight them. Just bring yourself back to focusing on your breaths. Inhale (count one), exhale. Inhale (count two), exhale. If you are limited for time, stop at the count of ten. Continue if time allows.

Congratulations. You have taken the first step in clearing your mind, releasing everyday stress, and opening up to the unlimited possibilities of your intuition.

10

Good Grief

I could hear the surf crash against the jetty wall as I sat watching television in the living room of our rented summer cottage. My son Drew lay sprawled across my lap, calling out, "Scratch me, scratch my legs, scratch my back."

The temperature was eighty-two degrees at midnight. It was the fourth day of this stifling heat wave. I'm certainly not complaining—I'll take the heat and humidity over three feet of snow and a windchill of ten below any day. My legs stuck to the vinyl rental furniture like pieces in the old Colorforms stick-and-play games.

Just before I fell asleep, I remember looking at the clock as it hit 2:22 AM. Usually, my dreams are very scattered and don't always make sense. This night, my dream was different. I was in some random house and there were a few familiar people milling about. My old boss and longtime friend, Tom, walked into the kitchen.

"Tom, what are you doing here?" I said with surprise. He kept smiling and didn't respond to my question.

"Why haven't you called me back?" I said. "I've sent you a couple of e-mails. It's not like you not to respond. Are you all right?

He continued to smile and reached out his hand to me. When my hand touched his, a flash of white light blinded my vision. Warm, fluidlike waves washed over my body. This euphoric feeling lasted only seconds. Tom hooked his arm in mine and guided me down a hallway. He finally spoke.

"Everything's fine. Don't worry about me. I'm okay."

He stopped, turned toward me, and gave me the best hug ever.

A tap on my shoulder woke me up. I jumped up and looked around the room. I was on the bottom bunk, sleeping next to my youngest son, Drew. He'd had a nightmare and called out to me in the middle of the night so, being half out of it, I had climbed into bed with him. He looked so peaceful, sleeping with his mouth half open, a small amount of drool perfectly pooled in the corner of his heart-shaped lips. Helplessly addicted to my Blackberry, I reached over to check the time and peek at my e-mail.

I was surprised to see an e-mail from an old friend at a Boston law firm I had worked in. When I clicked on it, a name on the second line caught my eye. Time stood still for that moment as I read it.

"Sad news. Late last night our dear friend Tom F. passed away. He was diagnosed in February with a brain tumor and went into hospice at the beginning of June."

I was in shock to read that my dear friend and mentor, Tom, had died. *A brain tumor?* I thought. *How can this be? Why didn't he tell me? I could have helped him. Wait a minute! How could I not have known?*

Then it dawned on me—the dream. In my shock of finding out someone so close to me passed, the dream I just woke from completely slipped my mind. For some unknown reason, Tom couldn't or didn't want to tell me he was sick. Yet, he knew he could come to me in a dream and I would be able to handle it much better. Yeah, right.

I quietly slipped out of bed so I wouldn't wake Drew. The sun was just starting to rise over the jetty. The sky was washed in a blend of watercolors: pale pink, mandarin orange, lavender, and fuchsia. It looked like Picasso had danced across the horizon with a paintbrush in each hand. Tiny diamonds sparkled on the water.

The ocean called to me, its energy drawing me closer as I walked down to the water's edge. I struggled with the thoughts in my head. I could feel how peaceful Tom was now, but I fought against the feeling. Wading into the crisp, clear water, I tasted salt on my cheeks, only it wasn't from the ocean; it was my tears. As I quietly wept and watched the surf, churning and tossing with the wind, I felt lighter. I rarely allow myself to grieve because my work is about death, and life after death, and about helping thousands of people find healing through their grief after a loved one passes. Usually, I have to be the strong and supportive one.

Now I found myself on the other side of the fence. I was actually grieving and desperately looking for signs. In practicing what I preach, I remembered there is no "on-demand" button for the other side. I should have learned this lesson once and for all after my friend Sharon passed away suddenly in the summer of 2009. I was devastated and in shock for weeks afterward.

Sharon's story is so very special to me. Several years ago, I got a call from a local radio station.

"Maureen, this is Sharon Santos from Fun 107 radio in Fairhaven. We got your name from Emily DeRosiers, one of our biggest fans. She said you would be a great addition to our 'Free Fortune Fridays' segments."

I chuckled to myself imagining me walking into the station with a crystal ball and dressed in Stevie Nicks's attire. This would be my big radio break. Although I was a bit nervous about doing it, I quickly agreed to appear on the show. Little did I know this was the beginning of not only an amazing friendship, but also a way to spread my message about hope and healing to a larger audience.

I'll never forget my debut day. There was a big snowstorm (and I hate to drive in the snow), so I left my house by 6:30 AM. I said several Hail Mary's as I went slip-sliding away down route 495. I asked all the dead people I know to help guide my car safely to the station. When I walked into the station, a young, dark-haired woman greeted me with a smile.

"Hi. I'm Sharon. You can come right over here and use this mic. Put on these headphones. We will record the calls so if you don't make a good connection, don't force it."

Sharon was so welcoming. My nerves settled down immediately. Her cohost, JR, gave me a hug and seemed very nice. Sharon and JR bantered back and forth on-air, with Sharon pretty much winning every round. She would jokingly tease him about anything and everything, live on the air.

"You all need to know how frail and brittle JR is. I'm worried his delicate frame won't hold him up. He's actually hunched over the microphone as we speak. He doesn't walk down the halls, he skips. I want all you listeners to picture Liberace."

Larry, the station manager and technician, had me rolling on the floor laughing. He did impressions and sound effects, and had a wit almost as quick as mine.

The hour segment flew by. I took many calls and did short, concise phone readings. I secretly renamed the show "Dialing the Dead." Some callers didn't get that I connected with the dead and just wanted to know about their love life. Others received beautiful messages from beyond, and some even came to see me for healing treatments after the show.

The last caller of the day introduced herself as Cheryl. Before she could even take her next breath, I felt her mother barreling in.

"I have your mom here for you. She's showing me a car accident."

Cheryl said, "Yes, I know what she's talking about."

"Boy, your mother is very pushy, Cheryl. Who has breast cancer?"

There was a long pause on the other end. I could hear sniffles in the background.

"I do. I'm battling stage 4 breast cancer. I can't believe my mother is telling you that. She must be upset because that's how she died. I was in a car accident last May. They were doing a CT scan of my back and found cancer in my bones and breast."

Thanks to that short on-air connection, Cheryl and I worked together for the next two years until her physical passing. And we remain close to this day. I remember her hobbling into my holistic healing office in so much pain and leaving practically skipping, with a beautiful smile that lit up the room.

Before I left the station that stormy January morning, Sharon confided in me that her aunt passed away from breast cancer so she held a special place in her heart for awareness and education about the disease.

Throughout the years, Sharon and I became close friends and confided in each other about life, love, and family. Sharon's mom, with whom she was extremely close, was diagnosed with lung cancer in 2003. At that time, I was traveling to southeastern Massachusetts—where Sharon's mom lived—quite often for home visits to the sick.

My sister Rosie and I would go to see Sharon's mom, J. I would do Reiki energy healing and acupressure, and Rosie did hypnosis (or attempted to) to help J deal with her anxiety. During one of our sessions, Rosie had J in a deep hypnotic state. Rosie's voice was putting me to sleep as I listened from the hallway. She could hypnotize a football team. Just as the hypnotic messages were being delivered, the phone rang. Now remember, J. is in a deep trance, but nevertheless she jumped up and grabbed the phone.

"Hello? Oh, good, and you? No, I'm not busy. What are you up to? Some lady is here and she's doing some hypnotizing thing, but I can talk. . . ."

It didn't help that I laughed so loud I snorted from the hallway. Rosie just rolled her eyes at me. Ironically, Sharon's mom's "angelversary" is the same day as our Sean Michael's. (An "angelversary," a term often used in the Children's Hospital cancer community in Massachusetts, is the date someone dies.)

It was hard for Sharon to talk about her mother without breaking down for quite a while after her passing. We would have deep conversations about death and the afterlife. Sharon shared with me her fear that she would die young from breast cancer. She said the only thing that would get her through such an experience was being able to see her mother again.

In the summer of 2009, Sharon was preparing to start her graduate program. She was so excited to get her master's in family counseling and to begin helping people. I was honored she asked me to give a recommendation for acceptance into the program.

In August 2009, Sharon apparently had a heart attack while she slept. She fought so hard to stay here and remained in a coma for two weeks. Then, this young, vibrant, feisty woman physically passed at the beginning of September 2009.

The day after Sharon's passing, she came to me in a dream. First, we were in a classroom and she was teaching young women how to walk for a beauty pageant (I found out after that she competed in pageants throughout her life). Then, she brought me into the next room. She ran to her mother and they were hugging each another and giggling. Sharon seemed so adjusted in such a short amount of time. I do believe that some people can actually sense that they might leave this earth at a young age.

My friend Tom used to say he thought he would die young like his father. I assured him that I saw him as an old man chasing his grandchildren around with his false teeth. Boy, was I wrong on that one.

Back at the beach cottage in the summer of 2010, I sat in front of the computer searching for any piece of Sharon and Tom to cling to. I brought up old e-mails and could actually hear their voices while I read them. I stared at photographs and listened to old voice mails. I asked them to visit me in dreams. It hit me one day when I was extra weepy . . . I was grieving. Despite knowing what I know, and all the thousands of experiences I've had connecting to spirit, *this* medium was being very *human*.

What I've learned from these experiences and the passing of my precious nephew, Sean, is that everyone grieves differently. As I am writing this, my chocolate lab, Ally, is doing her "Who Let the Dogs Out" dance. She crouches low to the floor, tipping her chocolate rump in the air, spinning in circles. It's as if she is showing off for a spirit. The thick, brown hair on the back of her neck stands straight up as she stops to look and bark at an empty space in the corner of my kitchen. Dogs and cats are very sensitive to spirits.

Even though I know we will all be together again one day, I do so terribly miss the physical part of my loved ones who are gone. For now, I'm embracing this *different* feeling—this grieving. Grief is always present; it just changes. I vow to live the best life I can in memory of my loved ones.

❦

As we travel through our lives, we are reminded that death and birth are parts of the natural cycle of life. The physical loss of a loved one is inevitable, but we can still grieve and pray that they never leave us. Each day I say a prayer for my parents, siblings, and immediate family that God hold them close to his heart . . . but not too close. I want us all to live forever, but I know that's not reasonable. I also know that we actually do live forever, because we are ultimately energy and energy can't possibly die. Neither can love. After all, we are all just spiritual beings having a physical experience this time around.

We have been given a superior gift—the ability to choose the attitude we'll adopt for the day. My cup isn't always half full as many would imagine. However, when it gets low, I find ways to fill it up. It is my choice to take the high road and work on being more positive, instead of wasting energy on negative comments, judgments, or anger. This life is too short. I choose to love unconditionally, cherish friends, and appreciate the beautiful family that supports me and surrounds me in love.

We have control over our thoughts, opinions, and actions (or inactions). Each day I redevote my energy to things I can change, impact, and learn from. I choose not to waste precious energy on things that are out of my control. It sounds easy, doesn't it? Well, it's always a work in progress. It takes patience and continuous shifting. When life hands you more challenges than you think you can take, be in each moment as it comes. And remember, this too shall pass.

11

Hollywood Hills

"Maureen? Elaine from Disney. We met a few years ago at a Buena Vista meeting and I never forgot you. I'd like to discuss a TV opportunity. . . ."

After listening to the full message, I took a deep breath and sat back in my chair. Two television possibilities in one day? Was it a full moon? I had passed many tests over the years with various production companies attempting to sensationalize my abilities. I prayed to my grandmother daily regarding my dream to spread my message about life after death, and the possibility of spirit communication, to a larger audience. This had been my dream for almost five years. I thought television would be the perfect avenue to achieve my goal.

Earlier in the day I had returned a call to Alex Rudd Productions. They produce a few popular reality television shows. Apparently, my friend John Holland, a well-known spirit medium, told them about me.

"We're considering you for a pilot for a new show featuring a man and a woman medium," one of Rudd's producers told me. "That's all we can tell you about the concept. We're all here in a meeting right now—everyone is here. We're going to have you bring through their dead spirits. Go ahead, Tony, step up to the speaker."

What was this, I thought. *Dialing the dead? Did they expect Grandpa to pop in with Sarah, the operator from Mayberry? "I've got a collect call from Gramps. Do you accept the charges?"*

Granted, I've been known to call myself the "overseas operator," but they were looking for the dead on demand!

I immediately felt a sinking feeling in my gut about this. An image of the show they were developing popped into my mind. I could see a panel similar to the one on *American Idol.* I couldn't quite tell if I was going to be a judge or the judged. The image ended with me telling a family that mom was coming through in spirit and although she sounded a bit "pitchy," she looked fantastic.

Since I was leaning toward not doing the pilot, it was easier to let my guard down and open the lines of communication. Suddenly, the room filled with spirits. It reminded me of the Verizon commercial where a large group of people gather in front of a house calling themselves the Network.

"I have your grandfather stepping forward, Tony. He says you never got to meet him. He's showing me a Navy ship and the tip of his finger is missing."

"Yes! Yes! That's my grandfather. He was in the Navy and while cutting meat, he cut the tip of his index finger off. Wow, I can't wait to tell my dad he came through."

"I now have a dad coming forward for the woman standing next to you, Tony."

There was silence on the other end of the phone. After a long pause, I heard a soft, shaky voice say, "Yes, that is probably *my* father. Is he saying anything?"

"He passed from a sudden heart attack and says he has three children: two boys and a girl."

"Oh my God, yes, he did have a heart attack. I'm one of three. Wow, I can't believe it. This is crazy."

The moderator of the call, a producer for the project, interrupted the "call from heaven."

"I'm sorry to cut this short, guys, but I think we have enough to make our decision. We will be in touch, Maureen."

I glanced down at the silent receiver. Maybe he had enough to satisfy his need to prove I was the real deal, but what was I supposed to do with all these spirits in midconnection, trying to get messages across to their loved ones? It was like losing power after a storm just before the Super Bowl.

I shut my eyes to ask the spirits to kindly leave. The hairs on my arm stood up as I felt a cool breeze in the room. Peeking out with one eye, I noticed the window was closed. *Where was the breeze coming from?*

I heard myself say aloud, "Thank you all for coming. I will pray that your loved ones here somehow get your messages. You might want to show up in a dream if you can swing it. The line is now officially disconnected."

The phone rang about an hour later. I looked down at the caller ID and saw "Alex Rudd Productions." My heart skipped a beat. My mind raced. *Yippee, I passed the test! Oh crap, they want me. Wait, they don't want me. They want to make money off me and sensationalize my abilities.* I let the call go directly to my answering machine.

"Maureen, this is Brandon from Alex Rudd Productions. We'd like to speak with you about coming out to L.A. next week to shoot the pilot for the project we talked about. Please call us back as soon as you can."

Looking back, I truly think this was a test. I felt a gentle nudge and trusted it was the God squad's way of guiding me in the right direction—I turned down the pilot.

An hour later I called my office to listen to messages. When I first heard Elaine's message from Disney, I thought someone was playing a joke on me. She mentioned that Disney was looking for a medium. By the end of her message, I realized it was no joke. She included names of executives I remembered from a meeting I had had with Buena Vista three years earlier with my dear friends and producers Marianne Leone and Dot Aufiero, who introduced me to the world of television.

I paced back and forth in my kitchen. I plunked myself down in my old brown recliner, holding the phone receiver in my hand. *I'll have to fly out and meet them,* I thought. *Will we have to move to L.A.? How will this affect our lives?* I took a few deep breaths, leaned forward in the chair, and carefully dialed the phone number. My heart pounded as I told myself, *Be cool. Try not to sound too excited. Breathe.*

My face felt warmer with each ring. The call went to voice mail. My body sank into the chair with disappointment. I left a brief message with several ways for Elaine to reach me. (I may have even left my gynecologist's number!)

I couldn't move from the chair. I burned a hole in the phone receiver just staring at it. *Please ring, please ring.* After almost two hours of waiting, I decided to give Elaine's offices another shot. And if the answering machine picked up again, I would try a different strategy.

"You've reached the office of . . ." When the message beeped, I started to leave a message. "Hi, Elaine. It's Maureen Hancock again. Sorry to bother you. I thought you should know I'm being represented by Paradigm Talent Agency." As I spoke, I heard a click and a live voice on the other end.

"Hey, Maureen, so good to hear from you! Do you remember a meeting a few years ago at Buena Vista? Some top executives at ABC wanted to try to do something with you, but couldn't quite put anything together?"

"Well, now we believe we have a concept you'll like and would like to go forward with development. We're looking for a strong woman who inspires others. Your show will be a docudrama following your life. Can you fly out to meet with our team as soon as possible?"

Everything slowed down as if in a dream. No sound came out of my mouth. I heard a giggle and realized it came from me. "Yes, of course I can fly out. I love the idea of following my life and all the hats I wear."

"Can you take me through a day in the life of you so I can get a sense of all those hats?" Elaine asked.

"I start my day by getting my boys ready for school. After dropping them off, I head to my office to see cancer patients and parents who have lost children. I offer these services free through my foundation Seeds of Hope. Sometimes I'm in hospitals and homes, helping the sick and their families with the final transition of life. I also assist private detectives with finding missing children, and help local police on a variety of cases, ranging from murders to vandalism. After picking the kids up at school, we do homework and head out to football. At night, I perform mediumship demonstrations at various venues as well as teaching mediumship. My day is chock-full."

"Wow," Elaine said. "I'm exhausted just listening to all you do. We'd love to get you out here. Let me know what works as far as scheduling and we'll arrange the meeting on our end."

After hanging up the phone, I had a million thoughts. *What will it be like with cameras following my family and me? I wonder how my husband and children will react.* I paused for a moment and realized what this all *really* meant: I had to clean my house!

I wanted to run outside and shout to the world that my dream was finally coming true. I had prayed daily that the right situation would present itself for me to spread my message beyond the south shore of Massachusetts.

This journey to spread the word through television had taken nearly five years. It began with a couple who had lost their only child,

Jesse, a magnificent light who continues to touch many lives with his eternal love and guidance. Jesse was an honor-roll student who loved to windsurf and write poetry. He also had severe cerebral palsy and was quadriplegic, unable to speak, and wracked by seizures. He died suddenly at the age of seventeen. This old soul came here to teach lessons of patience, understanding, insatiable laughter, and hope. Challenged within a body that couldn't always keep up with his brilliant mind, Jesse persevered and taught the medical community, as well as educational boards, to look beyond the body's shell.

After I did a reading for Jesse's parents, his mom said, "Maureen, you need your own television show. I'm calling my friend Dot. She's on the set of *The Departed*. She's an excellent producer and will want to meet you."

She left a message for Dot and about a week later we had a lunch meeting. Dot had just finished producing *Queer Eye for the Straight Guy*. She had some television connections but was more experienced in movie production. We moved forward with our plan to pitch a concept to various networks. We realized the concept needed to be "flushed out" a bit more, and we envisioned my doing events at restaurants, where I walked around the room giving messages from beyond. We called it "Dinner and Drinks with the Dead." The concept was similar to my evening presentations called "Postcards from Heaven," which I'd been offering for a few years.

Jesse's mom and Dot always believed in me. I am eternally grateful to both of them for sticking with me over the years and for being instrumental in making my dreams come true.

It was still dark when my alarm went off in the wee hours of June 2009. My bags were packed and waiting by the door. I slipped into my boys' room to kiss them good-bye. Tyler, my ten-year-old, looked so peaceful sleeping on his back with his blanket folded neatly under his chin. He typically stayed in the same position throughout the night. Drew, diagonally across from Tyler is his own little nook, was sprawled across his bed, his legs hanging over the side, blankets tangled around him and two pillows on the floor.

I tiptoed into my bedroom and whispered good-bye in my husband's ear. He opened one eye and wished me luck.

While driving to Logan Airport, I began to go over things in my mind I wanted to ask the Disney people. "How many hours a day will you be filming?" "Do I get to choose what's filmed?" "I would like to be as authentic as possible—no scripted situations. Is that possible?" "I don't want to end up like *Jon & Kate Plus Eight*, either. Okay?"

My mind was getting carried away.

The descent into Long Beach airport took my breath away. The sun had recently risen, and the sky looked brushed with pink and lavender hues. Butterflies fluttered in my belly as my excitement began to grow. Although I traveled alone, I felt surrounded by a band of angels and loved ones in spirit. A warm breeze tickled my cheek as I picked up my luggage at the outside carousel. Pins and needles ran up and down my legs. This always was a sign the spirits were all around me.

The traffic, normally very heavy on the 405, was exceptionally light, as if the God squad had cleared the way. I decided to treat myself for my birthday (Yes! It was my birthday, too!) and stay at a fabulous hotel—the Loews Santa Monica.

Walking up to the check-in counter, I envisioned being upgraded to a suite. I could see it in my mind . . . doors that opened to the gentle breezes of the ocean, long white curtains leading to a balcony, a cozy living room with a large cherry-wood desk, and a small kitchen.

The young man checking me in busied himself with looking at his computer the whole time I stood there. *Why won't he look up at me? Maybe if I smile or tell him it's my birthday he'll upgrade the room.* I even tried mental telepathy. I concentrated hard and squeezed my eyes shut, sending him positive thoughts: *Upgrade, upgrade . . .*

"Here you go, ma'am. You're in room 755. I hope you enjoy your stay." He handed me two room keys. I just stood there in a daze. *Hmm, I must be off today. Maybe it was just wishful thinking.*

As I turned to walk away, I heard, "Oh, and ma'am, you've been upgraded to an ocean-front suite." I quickly spun around. He smiled and looked directly into my eyes, almost as if he was in cahoots with someone. (Maybe my nephew Sean from beyond put the bug in his ear.)

The room was just as I'd imagined it, only a bit smaller. When I opened the curtains, the view took my breath away. To my right was the infamous Santa Monica Pier Ferris wheel. At night, the lights from the amusement ride would fill my room with dazzling flashes of blue, purple, and green.

A square patch of grass covered a small portion of the beach below. On it, a group of people were practicing tai chi. I couldn't tear my eyes away from their mesmerizing movements. As I watched, more people showed up on the beach, wearing less and less clothing! In fact, one

well-muscled man arrived on the scene wearing only a purple thong . . .
oh, and roller skates. A sign off to the left caught my eye . . . MUSCLE
BEACH. *Ahhh, I get it now.* I'd seen Muscle Beach in several movies over
the years. This was the place to see and be seen.

As much as I wanted to hang at the beach for the day with my sav-
age beige Irish tan (I burn, peel, and turn a pasty beige), the Disney
meeting was just a couple of hours away. I tossed my suitcase on the
bed and began sorting through my outfits. *Shall I wear the white pants
with a baby-blue shirt to accent my eyes or the sleeveless brown-and-black
pinstriped dress?* I wanted to make an impression, and because the pants
and shirt would need to be ironed, I chose the dress.

I plugged in my curling iron, and while I waited for it to get hot, I
applied a little more makeup than I normally would. Normally, I prefer
a more natural look, but I really wanted to wow them in this meeting.
I even went so far as to apply false eyelashes. My hand was shaking as
I attempted to attach the first one, and I ended up sneezing in midap-
plication. I was amazed to see that my nostril had grown a row of
eyelashes! I quickly fixed that, curled my hair, and headed downstairs.

I emerged from the elevator feeling glamorous and confident.
Standing there in the lobby, I felt a lot like a movie star and could sense
people's eyes on me. I even saw a few people point in my direction and
whisper. Now, I'm sure I had taken care of that false eyelash, so I could
only assume that I had succeeded in looking my best. In fact, three
valets tried to get my car at once. If they only knew that under all this
fabulous glamour was really a country bumpkin!

On my way to the meeting, a call came in from a friend I'd met in

L.A. a few years back who worked at 20th Century Fox.

"Hey, Maureen, this is Jim. I heard you were in L.A. Any chance you can stop by today? I want you to meet the vice president of television."

"Jim, hi! It's so great to hear your voice! I'm on Avenue of the Stars. If you're nearby, I can pop in for a little while. I'm about an hour early for my meeting."

Jim laughed. "This must be your lucky day. I'm at 2121 Avenue of the Stars. Stop in for a few minutes."

Fate was hard at work that day. I glanced to my left to find addresses and saw a big Fox sign up on the hill. I practically slammed on my brakes and headed into the parking lot. Jim, a tall, slim redhead with his Irish eyes smiling, was already in the lobby when I arrived. He quickly led me to the seventeenth floor.

"I really want you to meet this guy. He's so down-to-earth. I know you'll love him and he'll love you. He can give you advice about your meeting, and he has connections at other networks." Jim stopped at a corner office and poked his head inside. He looked back at me and said, "C'mon in," with a big Irish smile.

A tall, handsome, sharply dressed man in his late forties or early fifties walked over to me. "Hi, I'm Stephen," he said. "Don't I know you?"

There was an instant familiarity about this man. I felt it too. He asked about the Disney meeting (Jim had filled him in). About five minutes into the informal meet and greet, he put up his hand to stop the conversation. He was rubbing his chin with his hand and seemed to be in deep thought.

"Maureen, we're filming a new talk show for Fox. I want you to be in it as a special reoccurring guest. Can you come back next week to film thirty episodes?"

I think I slipped off the chair and almost tore my dress. *Holy crap! Holy crap! Look cool. Pull yourself together.*

"Well, my kids are on vacation next week, so I can only film for one day. Would one day of filming be alright?"

Stephen paused a moment. "Sure, that would be great. Whatever you can do is fine with me. I'm glad you put your family first. I knew I liked you. We can film eight episodes in one day and have you back with your family in no time."

I hugged Stephen and thanked him for giving me my first television opportunity. Jim and I walked out of the meeting with our mouths agape.

"In all my years at Fox," Jim said, "I've never seen anyone go into a meeting for a meet and greet and come out with an offer for a syndicated show." The shock on his face was priceless. "What just happened in there?"

I practically skipped to my car with Jim beside me, as we both laughed at the randomness of the morning. After giving me an awesome bear hug, he held both my shoulders, looked me in the eye, and said, "Kill it at your Disney meeting, Maureen. They'll love you as much as we all do."

As I pulled up to the Disney/ABC studios my eyes widened. A classic Mickey Mouse figure, the size of an oversized garage, smiled and waved his magic wand at me. I fumbled in my pocketbook for my camera, found it, and then focused in on Mickey.

"I'm sorry Miss, there are no photos allowed," came the security guard, seemingly out of nowhere.

I jumped as if I'd committed some sort of crime.

"You have to put your camera away," he continued. "I need your license and the name of the person you're here to see."

My mind went completely blank—a mammoth brain fart. For the life of me, I could not remember the vice president's name—a woman I had had numerous conversations with over the past few weeks. My face turned bright red from embarrassment (not to mention the fact that, well, I'm supposed to be psychic!).

I fumbled for my license while wracking my brain for her name. The guard looked at me a little dubiously and noticed my shaking hand as I offered him my license. Just when I thought he was about to give up on me, her name popped into my head. "Elaine Metaxas!" I blurted.

He checked his computer, then directed me to the parking area, and instructed me to check in at the reception desk once inside the building for permission to go up to the fifth floor.

I parked but wasn't quite ready to get out of my car. I reapplied my lipstick in the rearview mirror, checked on the placement of my eyelashes, fluffed my hair a bit, and then sat there for a few minutes taking deep, cleansing breaths . . . well, I was attempting to breathe. Truth is, I could barely do it. I kept repeating, "Breathe, breathe. I'm at the ABC building!"

I said a little prayer, asking for all my angels, guides, deceased loved ones, saints, God, Jesus, Mary, and my dead Shetland sheepdog, Jillian, to accompany me to this meeting and help it go smoothly. As I prayed,

I felt my confidence growing. Then I courageously got out of the car and headed toward the building, followed by my spirit entourage.

When the elevator opened on the fifth floor, a cheerful-looking woman was leaning against a cubicle wall, talking to a colleague. She glanced over at me and our eyes locked. I instantly felt comfortable in her presence and hoped she was the person I would be meeting with.

"Maureen? Elaine. It's so great to see you again!" My natural instinct was to hug her, but I just reached out to shake her hand. Elaine's assistant, Arielle, showed me to the waiting area. As I sat on one of the small, hard couches, my head began to throb. Spirit loved ones for the people I would be meeting with started to communicate with me: "Hello, Blondie. I'm Ryan's grandfather. Make sure you tell him I'm here, okay?" "Hey, I'm his grandmother, Mary. I'm sure he'd much rather talk to me. Please tell him I hear his prayers."

My hands started to get clammy and I was having heart palpitations. My mouth was as dry as the Sahara. I could barely move in my form-fitting dress. My stomach started to growl loudly. *Please, God, don't let me have gas bubbles. My outfit is too tight, and I'm afraid this material isn't flame retardant.*

Because of my connection to an L.A. talent agency we had used for previous network meetings, I reached out for representation for this meeting. Chris, a tall, young, thirtysomething agent was sent to the Disney offices to sit in. Just then he arrived.

"Sorry I'm late. I went to the old ABC offices. I didn't realize they'd changed buildings," Chris panted, with sweat beads dripping down his forehead as he approached me in the waiting area. "Here's what we're going to do. I'm going to just sit back and listen to what they have to say. You wow them with what you do, and we'll talk after the meeting."

Arielle poked her head around the corner. "We're ready for you. Please follow me."

We were led into Elaine's office. I grabbed a corner of the pinkish-red couch and carefully sat down. Chris sat next to me. The person sitting in a chair to the right of me kept smiling and quickly stood up to introduce himself. *Oh my,* I thought, *he looks just like Perez Hilton.*

"Hi, I'm Ryan, a producer working with Elaine." My mouth dropped and I rolled my eyes.

"Are you alright? What's wrong?"

"Your grandparents were hanging out with me in the waiting area. Is your grandmother's name Mary?"

He gasped and held his chest. His hazel, puppy-dog eyes filled up as he slowly nodded his head yes.

I leaned over and held his arm. "I'll tell you more about them later. She is one strong lady," I whispered in his ear. The woman sitting to Ryan's right, Rebecca, started to giggle nervously when she heard what I whispered to Ryan.

Elaine went right into talking about the concept.

"We are superexcited about working with you, Maureen. We're changing one of our networks to include more docudramas and reality television. We think you're the perfect fit for a flagship show for the new lineup for the network. We're very interested in how you live

your life—balancing motherhood, your charity work, and most especially, your large, close-knit Irish-Catholic family. We know you can
give hope to so many in these trying times."

The door swiftly opened and in walked a small-framed man with
glasses. He seemed to be in a rush. Elaine and Ryan sat up and nervously moved forward in their seats. *Hmmm, this must be someone
important. I wonder if he knows he looks like John Lennon.*

"I'm David." He hesitantly reached out his hand to me. Tempted to
grab it and yell, "Boo!" I resisted the temptation. I smiled and introduced myself.

Elaine continued. "David, I was just filling Maureen in on our idea
for her own show and how excited we are for her to join our network."

I couldn't quite get a good read on David. He just sat back in his
chair, chewing on his pen and staring at me. I stood up and took them
through a day in the life of me, swinging my arms, jumping around,
and just being my goofy self.

David leaned forward in his seat and finally spoke. "Why do you
want a TV show, Maureen?"

What? I thought. *Me? A TV show? Why did I want a show? Didn't they
want me? Isn't it the other way around? Think fast. No, wait, don't think.
Breathe, reach down into your heart, and just speak your truth. What's that
thumping noise? Oh, it's my heart pounding against my chest. Here goes . . .*

I leaned forward and looked directly into David's kind eyes. "I want
my own show so I can reach out to as many people as possible, to help
them, to plant seeds of hope where they're needed. I want to be the teacher
in a world that has so much pain, grief, and despair. I want to show people

that we are so much more than this physical body, so they can live each day like it might be their last. I want people to examine their own lives and know how important it is to pay it forward, forgive, laugh, come together as family, and realize that the person next door might just need a hand."

Everyone in the room stayed silent for what seemed like forever. I walked over to David.

"David, ask yourself what you do to give back to others? Is it enough? It's not all about how much we have or how many cars are in our driveway. It's about figuring out why we are really here, finding joy again, and living the best life we can until we go."

David's eyes widened. He uncrossed his legs and sighed as he sat back in his chair. He slowly began to smile and his eyes lit up. I could see a twinkle in his eye as if he'd just discovered the meaning of life. He cleared his throat and said softly, "Okay. Thank you."

David stood up and hugged me. It totally took me by surprise. Warmth filled my body from head to toe, and I had my own realization at that moment. *These are the people I would like to work with.* I knew God was telling me they were the right fit for me. As much as they needed to make money for the network, my intuition told me there was a higher power at work here . . . someone bigger than any president of a network.

I signed a four-year option with ABC/Disney for my own reality television show. I was overjoyed with the outcome. In June 2010, the executive producers of the *Ghost Whisperer,* Ian Sander and Kim Moses, signed a deal with ABC Media Productions to executive produce my show. I am still pinching myself on that one.

A week after my big Disney meeting, I headed back to L.A. from Boston to film the eight episodes for Fox that I had committed to at my recent meeting with the vice president. I cleared this appearance through Disney as my contract was exclusive for reality television only.

· It was so surreal to drive up to the Fox studio lot and give my name—and actually have the little arm lift up to let me in. It was scorching hot by 9 AM. I parked the car and went to the building I was told to show up at for hair and makeup. When I walked in, the staff directed me down the hall to a small room. When I got to the room, there were signs for *Divorce Court* with Judge Toler everywhere. I was in the wrong place. Yup, I could hear everybody now: "Did you hear the psychic got lost and was late for the taping? What a hoot!"

I snuck out a back door and went across the parking lot to another building. I prayed to my guardian angels to help me find my way. I heard in my head, "Go to building 11."

When I opened the double-glass doors, a woman rushed up to me and said, "Are you Maureen the medium? We have ten minutes for hair and makeup. Please run with me." She took my arm and we started running down a long hallway. I was whisked through hair and makeup. A tall bald man holding a walkie-talkie took me by the arm and took me to another room.

"This is your dressing room, Maureen. If you need anything, let me know. I am one of the production assistants. Please change into one of the outfits hanging in the bathroom, and we'll be back to get you in five minutes. Your first episode starts in ten minutes.

My dressing room was fabulous! A long, plush brown couch lined the back wall and two dark brown, oversize leather chairs filled the corners of the room. The table was covered in various snacks and drinks. I stuffed a couple of granola bars in my pocketbook for later. I felt like I was in a dream. I opened the door to peek out and saw something I missed on my way in. The door had a sign on it that read: MAUREEN HANCOCK, EXPERT WITNESS. What was I an expert witness about? Maybe this was a mistake.

I quickly changed into a beautiful pair of light gray pants with a purple top. As I was putting on my necklace, there was a loud knock on the door.

"We're rolling in five. We need you now!"

I opened the door and started running. That seemed to be the pace around here. I was led down a few flights of stairs to the basement. Behind the set were the props, lighting, sound, and production areas. A short, dark-haired woman quickly set me up for sound, attaching a small box that looked like an old Sony Walkman to my backside. As she was running the cord under the front of my shirt, I got up the guts to ask her a question.

"What is this show about anyway?" She stopped what she was doing and stared at me like I had two heads.

"Nobody told you the concept of the show?"

"No," I answered sheepishly.

"It's about engaged couples who think they are ready to get married but have concerns. Relationship expert Dr. Michelle Callahan questions them and decides if they are ready. What are you an expert in?"

"Um, talking to dead people," I whispered.

She quipped back, "Well, isn't that special."

So, my first experience in television was sort of like a blind date. I had no idea what I was doing, who I was meeting, or what the outcome would be. My psychic switch was turned off, until I heard my name announced by the host of the show. The bright lights shined in my eyes and the cameras moved to focus on me. I was sitting in the front row of the audience. I felt relatively calm considering this was my first time being filmed for a nationally syndicated television show.

During each of the episodes I was on as an "expert witness," a couple was dealing with the loss of a loved one. I was called upon to shed some light on the situation and give messages from beyond. Each time my validations got stronger and stronger.

The show aired for a few months in several test market cities around the United States. I had my own "Hollywood" viewing for all my friends and family back home. The show was then picked up for an additional three months but was canceled after its first season. I received hundreds of e-mails from viewers around the country after my episodes aired. People were looking for connections with loved ones who had passed and for psychic advice regarding their relationships.

❧

Patience! It's not an easy lesson for me because I'd prefer life to happen on *my* timing. But I have come to realize that divine timing usually wins. (No, make that always wins.) When you have a dream that you are truly excited about, it can be hard to have faith and trust that it will come about. But much goes on behind the scenes that we don't know about and can't do anything about. We have to wait. And while we are waiting, we have the opportunity to get even clearer about our desires. Don't settle for less than what you desire. Give the universe an opportunity to sculpt your dream perfectly for you. It always will . . . unless you give up on it. Don't give up!

Consider the growth of a bamboo tree. It usually takes a full three years in the ground before any growth appears at all. During that time, its roots are growing deeply underground. Then, as if by magic, the tree may grow up to four feet in a twenty-four-hour period!

Think about a dream you have. Have you given up on it because you haven't seen any signs of it coming to fruition? Or did someone tell you that it's a pipedream, that you're crazy? Did someone else give you a hundred reasons why your dream wouldn't work. Don't let anyone take the wind out of your sails.

As you become clearer about what your dream looks and feels like, trust that it will come to be. Keep your focus on you desire, rather than on the fact it hasn't shown up yet. Trust that it will! I believe in you.

12

Psychic Children

When I was a child, seeing and hearing spirits in my bedroom and milling about my home was a nightly occurrence. Oftentimes, I would keep these encounters to myself in fear I would be taken back to the hospital, as my sister hammered home at the time. It was a lonely place to be as a child with nobody to talk to about what I was experiencing.

When the spirits first started to appear, I was cautiously curious. Patrice and Sarah, the sisters I shared a room with, would be fast asleep when the "ghosts" came. Having spent so much time in the hospital, my sleep was erratic and constantly interrupted. I was ultrasensitive to noise and movement.

I stopped talking about the spirits when my parents and siblings dismissed my visions or chalked them up to the medication I was taking for the lead-paint poisoning. Looking back, I wish someone had explained to me what was happening. I now believe having been in a coma and so close to death when I was young opened a portal to the other side.

I'm amazed at the number of psychic or sensitive children speaking up today. It makes me happy to know these children are not keeping their gifts to themselves, as I did as a child. The first step in helping your child understand what is happening to him or her is for you, the parent, to accept and understand it. There are hundreds of books on psychic or sensitive children, as well as television shows like *Psychic Kids: Children of the Paranormal,* which openly discuss and help parents guide their intuitive or gifted children. Discussing psychic phenomenon and the paranormal is much more mainstream today than when I was young.

Throughout my work over the years, I have met some incredibly gifted children who are very sensitive and open to intuition or visions. In fact, most children have a very strong psychic sense, often seeing (clairvoyance) and hearing (clairaudience) their deceased loved ones, especially if they've never met them. How many times has your little one mentioned they have an imaginary friend? Ask your child questions about this friend, such as: "What's your friend's name? What do they look like? Are they saying anything to you?"

You just might be surprised by the answers. Maybe their "imaginary friend" is actually a loved one in spirit.

Many of my clients have told me their children tell them they see someone in the corner of the room, and the child may smile for no reason. That "someone" may be a spirit playing with the child or making them laugh.

Naturally, as children get older, they sense it's not as accepted to be hearing voices or seeing imaginary people. Many people have been conditioned to think having this ability is weird, scary, or maybe even crazy. But intuition, visions, and psychic abilities—all part of the psychic sense—are a God-given gift and innately inherent in each individual. It's up to parents to teach their children, as well as themselves, to embrace this ability or control it, rather than be afraid and fearful.

I remember when I started first grade, I told my new friend, Debbie about the people that came to visit me at night. We were sitting next to a huge oak tree at recess. She laughed right in my face and shouted through the playground, "Maureen has ghosts in her house! Run away!" A group of my classmates got up and started squealing and running from me. Nobody would come near me for about a week. I felt like an outcast—like I had cooties. I pretended to be sick every day and would go to the nurse, just so I could go home.

I often receive e-mails from parents seeking guidance on how to help their children who are having visions and encounters with spirit. Here's an example of a recent e-mail I received:

Maureen, please help me. My children see people who have passed. My girls can see things; they are triplets and they are only nine years old. I just want to be sure they are seeing good spirits. One of my daughters saw a woman today and described her; I have no idea who she is. My daughter doesn't know how to interpret what she sees or what the messages might be. My girls are a little bit freaked out about what's happening to them. Let me know if you can help at all, please."

Just because you are feeling completely wigged out, your child doesn't need to know this. Acknowledge that your child is having real encounters with spirit. Tell them they are not imagining things, and they are not alone either. Help them feel normal by telling them many other children are sensitive too.

Help them to embrace this ability by encouraging them to express themselves freely when a psychic event happens. You might say, "Have you seen Papa today? What did you two talk about? Did he say or do anything funny?"

If your children seem upset or scared about their abilities, talk about it. Ask them, "What is scaring you the most about what you're sensing? Do the spirits only come at night or do you see them during the day?"

If you notice that the spirit or energy is waking them up at night, talk to your child about control. Psychic ability can be like a light switch, and with the right guidance, your child can be taught to turn it off when it's too overwhelming. Tell them, "You're protected by the angels. Ask all the angels to come in and surround you. St. Michael the Archangel is your protector. Call on him when you need him. Tell the spirits to leave you alone if they are bothering you. Try to say it firmly and try your hardest not to be afraid. The spirit probably likes that you can sense them, so they are reaching out because you're so special."

If you have more than one child, you might notice that it's your ultrasensitive child who has the most profound abilities. That child is usually the peacekeeper of the family, the one other children flock to, the one who sticks up for the underdog.

I recognize these unique abilities in my own children. Tyler and Drew, especially when they were younger, always talked about seeing their cousin Sean and described what he was doing in great detail. A few years back, during one scorching summer afternoon, the kids and I took a stroll to meet Sean's family at the cemetery. We know our Sean isn't really "there"—in fact, he goes with us to "visit"!

This became very clear when we headed back to my house that summer day. Rosie and John, Sean's parents, and his sister, Stassia, came with us. We were all sprawled on the couch, exhausted from the heat, while Tyler and Drew played on the floor. I casually asked Tyler if he ever saw Sean. Tyler had known Sean physically, and suddenly, it was apparent he knew Sean in spirit just as well. And at that moment Tyler replied, "Yeah, he was just throwing pies at Rosie, Stassia, and Ally (the dog)."

We all gasped, "What?" Rosie, John, and Stassia shot up from the couch. Tyler/Sean were echoing the words of someone who had come to Rosie and John's house earlier that day.

Just that morning, their UPS driver came to the door to drop off a package. Their home was flooded regularly with letters, flowers, food, and donations to Sean's scholarship fund, which helps kids in the community. Their UPS driver came to know the family very well, and he was particularly friendly with John.

The three adults spoke on John's front porch that morning. The UPS driver had physically lost his son years ago too and related to their grief. Wanting to help, he excitedly and graciously offered the idea to host a fund raiser for Sean in the next few months. He was going to hold it at the town hall, expecting they could get as many as a few hundred to a thousand people to attend. He made Rosie and John promise to keep his plan under their hats since it hadn't been finalized and he needed to get the town's approval first. Rosie and John agreed, silently nodding their heads. "We won't tell anyone."

They started to head back into the house, when John suddenly called out, "Hey, what are we going to do there anyways?"

The UPS driver replied, "I figured there are enough people in town who would want to throw a pie in my face. I'll charge them ten bucks."

My children would often talk about Sean as if he were still with us. They could do this openly because I taught them that the spirit or soul survives a physical passing. As they have become older, the conversations with Sean have lessened, but their belief and curiosity regarding the afterlife is ongoing.

My younger son, Drew, asks many questions about death and dying. I worry his fascination with death is causing anxiety. When I was reading a book to him before bed recently, he looked up at me with his big, inquisitive, blueberry eyes and asked, "Mom, what if you die? How will I know you're still here?"

I reached over and hugged him so tight. I whispered in his ear: "You will know I'm still here because I promise to show you. You'll hear my voice in your head giving you guidance. I will come in your dreams. I will use music to play you songs, and the wind to brush your cheek. I will call your name when you least expect it."

"Mom, you can't die. I need you. When I get married I want you to live in my cellar."

I continued to hold him and assure him that death is not the end, and he didn't need to worry about that right now. He drifted off to sleep clinging to my arm.

My friend, Noelle, has a very intuitive twelve-year-old daughter who constantly sees spirits. Maddie is working through embracing her ability and learning not to be afraid of the spirits. She recently reached out to me for some guidance. When she was a bit younger, she only saw passed relatives. Now, she has visions of people she doesn't even know, even when she's in the car with her mom. She will see them sitting on the side of the road, poking their head out from behind a tree, and at sporting events.

I asked Maddie to share her story in the hopes it helps another young child identify and feel normal. Here's Maddie's story, in her own words:

When I was about three years old, my grandfather passed. My grandfather and I were very close. About a year or so after he passed, he would come to visit me. My mother tells me that she will never forget the day we were all sitting at the kitchen table. I told her how my grandfather thought my baby brother was so handsome and so beautiful. My mom, never mind the rest of my family, seemed a little surprised at the way I told her—I guess with using my grandfather's exact words—and because he never met my little brother. But I could see him. I could talk to him. When my mom asked me where I got these words from, I simply pointed up toward the sky, smiling, and said my grandfather was in the clouds telling me these things. About five years later, my great-grandmother passed. The weekend after she passed, I was sick. That's when I saw her in the rocking chair sitting next to me. It was Super Bowl Sunday. My nana never missed a Super Bowl.

When my mom came upstairs to check on me, she heard me talking to my great-grandmother. I told her what my nana had said. Nana told me she was okay and happy to be with my great-grandfather. After that, every once in a while, I would see a relative I would recognize and I would tell my parents. Over the past few weeks, I have been seeing people and animals that no one else can see. It doesn't matter where I am—at the mall, walking down the street, in my living room, or at my friend's house. They find me.

Most of my family is sensitive, and for me to have the "gift" is very exciting. But sometimes when I see something, there are people around, and I can't really say anything. One tip Maureen gave me has been very helpful. She said, "You're the one in control. Sometimes you have to be the one to say, 'Go away. I don't want you right now.'" I'm so lucky that I have grown up in an environment with people who do understand what I'm going through and know how to help me deal with it.

Psychic gifts in children show up in many ways. The most common gifts I see in children are clairsentience, clairvoyance, and telepathy. Sensitive children tend to feel (clairsentience), see (clairvoyance), and pick up the thoughts of another (telepathy).

The ability to feel is also known as the gift of empathy. This means that a person with this psychic sensitivity has the capability to sense, feel, and take on the physical emotions of others, including animals or even spirits.

I was very empathic as a child. While other kids in the neighborhood played kickball and hide-and-seek, my friend, Jackie, and I volunteered at the local nursing home. We were only eleven years old. I always felt so bad that many of these elderly folks had nobody to visit them. Their eyes would light up when we walked into the room.

It's helpful for the parents of sensitive children to learn all they can about the various types of psychic abilities so they can help their children understand and cultivate these gifts. Take it from me, your child will feel isolated and alone if you try to ignore their calls for help because of your own fears of the unknown.

&

Help your children understand death. Tell them death is not the end; it is simply a transition from one place to another, sort of like walking from the kitchen to the living room. When someone dies, all that happens is they simply change forms. They aren't "gone"; they are simply transformed. They transition from a physical body to a more subtle-energy body. You might tell children simply that they change from a human body to an angel body.

Imagine the life of a flower. A flower starts as a hard, dense seed. Then, at some point, it breaks free from its encasing and transforms into a soft, subtle flowering bloom. The essence of the flower is there both in its dense seed form and in its flowering form. Same thing, just different forms. Death is exactly the same. Our essence, our soul—who we really are—breaks free from our physical encasing (our body) and moves into a subtler form, which some very sensitive people can still see, especially children and those about to pass.

One of the most important things you can do as the parent of a sensitive child is to work through your own fears about death, so that your children don't associate death with stereotyped images like haunted houses, ghosts, and evil spirits.

Giving children a foundation based on love and truth—as opposed to fear— will keep them content, empowered, and happy.

Having a support system in place is also key in helping children and teens deal with their sensitivities. Teens who recognize they are having detailed visions, intuitive hits, premonitions, and dreams about passed loved ones need to have open and clear communication with parents and others who are experiencing the same thing.

Intuitive teens have a huge weight on their shoulders, especially if they share their special abilities with friends. Add to that the fact that their hormones are raging and anxiety is high. Then throw in medium and psychic skills, and you have an overwhelmed teen on your hands. I've noticed many sensitive teens don't know what to do with all the energy running through their system so it starts to manifest as an anxiety or depressive disorder. Help them understand it's very helpful to talk to a trained therapist about this. Many psychologists are open to holistic and natural ways to assist gifted children and teens.

There's a fabulous place right here in Massachusetts called A Place of Light. It is a center dedicated to helping families understand and embrace intuitive children. It was featured on an episode of *Psychic Kids* on A&E. My friend Jill Sylvester is a certified counselor and integrates traditional and alternative forms of treatment for gifted and sensitive children.

Most important, know you are not alone out there. The stigma of having special abilities is wearing off in society, and I feel many gifted children (and their parents) are reaching out for answers, guidance, and acceptance. Take the first step to empower yourself and your family to understand, nurture, and appreciate your God-given gifts.

13

To Live For

I have a question for you: Do you picture me in my den holding séances until 3 AM or brewing potions in my kitchen? If so, I'd better dispel that myth. I once mentioned during a show that I took my child to the doctor and a woman exclaimed, "Oh my God, *you* have children?"

"Two boys."

"I know it sounds odd, but I thought you spent all your time helping people."

Yes, I help people *and* I have a family—like the 71 percent of moms who work. I do try to keep my home life separate from my work. It might surprise you, but when I'm home, after helping my sons with their homework and throwing in a load of laundry, I plunk myself in front of the TV to watch *Jerseylicious* or *The Bachelor*.

While I specialize in helping people connect to their departed loved ones, people seem to think I have a full handle on the unseen. They ask me to find their missing loved ones, locate lost jewelry, diagnose medical problems, talk to sensitive children, and discover if their partner is cheating. They think they've found Dr. Phil, the Supernanny, and the Ghost Whisperer, all rolled into one.

Do I find my work challenging? At times I do. I suffered panic and anxiety attacks throughout my childhood and off and on during adulthood. As a sensitive intuitive, I pick up on other people's grief and negative energy. I've learned to protect myself and create some distance, and I need to set limits with people—especially when they're so wrapped up in what *they* want they don't see *my* vulnerabilities right in front of them.

Connecting to spirit can drain your energy if you are not careful. I have to raise my energy to a level that holds a connection to spirit for long periods. Things that help me raise my energy include going to the gym, meditation, eating a healthy diet (no red meat, no alcohol), and getting plenty of rest.

For years, my presentations lasted four to five hours. Seeing all those sad faces looking back at me yearning for that one last hug from heaven kept me going like the Energizer Bunny. Over the past year, I've started to be more aware of my energy reserves and how much I can give. Case in point . . .

I did a show at Albert's restaurant in Stoughton, Massachusetts, four years ago for more than 200 people. The readings started at 7 PM.

Just after midnight, headed toward my last table, the vision in my right eye weakened. I saw a zigzag pattern of light that started small and then took over both eyes—like looking into a kaleidoscope. Half the room looked black to me, and then I fell to the floor. I found out later that this was an ocular migraine. I get them quite often now after performing for large audiences.

You might think that nearly passing out at the end of a show would help me realize I need to slow down and take better care of myself. But it took a serious case of diverticulitis to wake me up and make me understand I could not continue at that pace.

Just before leaving my home to do a house party in 2006, I felt sharp pains in the lower left side of my stomach. These weren't just your typical gas pains—they caused me to stop in my tracks and double over, whimpering in agony. But with my "disease-to-please" resolve in full force, I didn't cancel the house gathering. Instead, I called my sister Rosie and asked if she could come with me.

"Rosie, would you mind driving me to my house party tonight?"

"What's wrong? Your voice sounds funny. Are you okay?"

"Well, um, I'm in severe pain and I don't think I can drive."

"Can't you cancel the party, Mo? My God, you can't keep up this grueling schedule. They'll understand."

I lined up the excuses for going on: "These people took the night off from work. Some are traveling long distances. One woman flew in from Virginia."

Rosie was silent on the other end of the phone. She wasn't buying it, but she knew my resolve. "I'll be right over," she promised.

By the time we reached our destination, beads of sweat were forming on my temples and my face was flushed. Rosie held her hand to
my forehead.

"You feel really hot, Mo. Maybe you shouldn't go in."

"Oh, my God, no. I have to. I can't bear the thought of disappoint-
ing all these people. They've waited six months for this party."

"Okay, but if you still look like this after the show, I'm taking you
to the hospital."

Before starting the readings, I excused myself and went into the
bathroom. There I begged, prayed, and looked to the heavens for help
in getting me through the night. I called on any dead person that
would listen, pleading with them to take my pain away so I could help
their loved ones in the other room.

My connections most of the night were beyond exceptional. When
I spoke, I felt like it wasn't my voice coming through. It was as if I had
floated out of my pain-filled body and let someone else do all the work.
In between readings, I doubled over in pain.

Typically, I sit across from the person I'm reading for and hold their
hands—this helps make the connection stronger. In my head, I ask any
"special guest" spirits to step forward. I then feel a connection start to
brew. My head tingles and I hear voices inside my mind. My heart races
and I feel anxious. When I know I have a good link, I interview the spirit
and ask questions (mind to mind, just with my thoughts): "Who are
you? Can you give me a name? How did you pass? Let me feel how you
passed on my body. Did you have children? What message can I relay?"

Toward the end of that night, my readings became shorter and more of a struggle to deliver—I could barely finish. Why didn't anyone suggest I go home or head to the nearest emergency room? Because the people who come to connect with me are so entrenched in their own pain they can't see mine. I thought I would never get to the finish line. When the last reading was completed, and I was doubled over in pain, a woman approached me as I put on my coat.

"I really wanted to hear more from my husband," she told me. "I'm surprised he didn't have more to say. If he's still here, can you ask him why he wouldn't talk to me more?"

My wiseass self wanted to say, "Well, he didn't really want to talk to you when he was alive; why would he talk to you now?" Instead, I took her hands in mine and looked her in the eye and said, "I gave as much as I could and he said what he needed to say."

Rosie gunned it to Brockton Hospital. I worried when they skipped the waiting room and wheeled me immediately into radiology for a CT scan of my abdomen. Feeling completely wiped out, my intuitive antenna was down, and I couldn't pick up anything on my condition. (It's much easier for me to get information on others, rather than on myself.)

After the scan, the doctor came back to see me in less than twenty minutes. "You have an acute case of diverticulitis," he told me. "It could have been caused by something you ate or by excessive stress. We're going to start you on a few different antibiotics, but we also have a team of surgeons standing by if the antibiotics don't work. Are you allergic to anything?"

Rosie glared at me. I wasn't sure if she was reacting to the comment about stress or about being allergic to anything. She knows I'm completely stressed out with my work, *and* that I'm allergic to every antibiotic I've ever taken.

The doctor continued. "If we can get your fever down and pump you full of antibiotics, there's a chance we won't have to operate. You're awfully young to be experiencing this condition at your age. What do you do for work?"

Oh, the dreaded question. At that time in my life, it was hard for me to come right out and say I was psychic or I spoke with the dearly departed. My answer would usually be, "I own a holistic healing center and I have a cancer foundation where I work with the sick."

"I'm a massage therapist," I said this time, under my breath. (By the way, today it doesn't take me long to come clean and say, "I'm a medium. I talk to the dead." I get a kick out of the big eyes and look of surprise I get with this statement. I'm no longer uncomfortable sharing what I do.)

The antibiotics worked and I avoided surgery. This was a huge wake-up call for me to slow down. I needed to take better care of myself and do things that made me happy. Several hours later, while wheeling me to her car from the hospital lobby, Rosie asked, "What makes you happy, Moey?"

"Helping other people, being with my family, and helping out my friends make me very happy."

"No, that doesn't count right now. What makes *you* happy? What can you do just for you?" Rosie asked.

I paused for a moment. My answer shocked me. "I don't know." I was so busy trying to help others, I got lost in my own shuffle.

I now look at every day as an opportunity to grow and continue working on myself. I'm more aware of how negative energy affects me and my ability to be a clear channel for spirit communication. Most of the real battles we face are inside us, and one of mine was putting me first. I'm reminded again of a time after my sister Rosie's son, Sean, passed.

Rosie would call me each morning to check in with Sean, and I would be my goofy self and make her laugh until we both cried. Sean would never let us down—always coming through with something to lift our own spirits.

During one of these morning calls I said, "You need to get out of the house. What do you want to do?"

"I don't really feel like doing anything," Rosie answered. "I think I'll just stay in bed and meditate."

"Meditate, shmeditate—get your Irish arse out of bed and let's do something."

"Okay. The only thing I feel like doing is eating a brownie sundae," Rosie said.

Brownie sundaes became Rosie's drug of choice, as we weren't much into drowning our sorrows in booze, riding into the sunset on Harley's, or smoking unfiltered cigarettes. We are connoisseurs of good food.

Later that day, hot, gooey chocolate fudge oozed off my spoon as I indulged in the first bite of my warm brownie sundae from Skinners

Sugar House, our local down-home ice cream parlor and candy shop.

"Yum, this is to die for," I said. Next to me sat Rosie, her golden hair waving beautifully with the wind, her eyes focused on the prize: chocolate, of course. We were sitting on a wooden park bench, under a magnificent chestnut tree. It was peaceful and calm. The quiet chirping of birds filled the air.

"Correction," said Rosie. "It's to *live* for."

She's right. I want to *live* for those moments . . . not just the chocolate highs, but also the taking time out of my busy day to be with people I love. After Sean passed, Rosie found ways each day to create tiny joy-filled moments to live for.

Just recently, I logged on to give my daily inspiration on Facebook. Rosie's post was the first to capture my attention and struck a chord in my heart: "Joy is the greatest cleanser, and it is the greatest testimony to our faith" (St. Francis of Assisi).

Rosie could have been one of those people who just coil into a ball of grief, pulling the covers high over her head. She could have wound up posting some putrid, mundane saying like, "Same shit, different day." Instead, she lifted the shade one day and felt the warmth of the sun. She took the next step and used all her remaining strength to open the window. A warm breeze caressed her face and a butterfly danced across the window screen, as if to say, "I left my cocoon to find a whole new world out here!"

Rosie instinctively knew the butterfly relayed a message from Sean through its fairylike dance that day. In accepting its newfound vehicle, the butterfly nudges us to trust in the inevitable journey of change in our lives. Transitions come in all shapes and sizes, and Sean's was of epic proportions for our family, especially his devoted, doting mother. Now she knows that when her physical journey in this incarnation ends, she will soar with Sean on the wings of love.

Back at Skinners, my head starts to pound. Maybe I inhaled the sundae a bit too fast. Brain freeze! I placed my thumb against the roof of my mouth to relieve the pain. I looked over at Rosie and couldn't see her face. She was nose deep in her sundae, scraping every last bit out of the cup. I lost it. I started that laugh you get in church as a child and can't stop. Or, better yet, that laugh you get when someone you know slips and pratfalls in front of you. (My Aunt Peggy has that disorder. She can't help it.) I laughed so hard a walnut shot out of my mouth and disappeared into Rosie's thick hair. It would take days to find it and a ground-search supervisor to oversee the process! (Rosie is blessed with long, curly hair, but on humid days, it can expand to resemble Animal from the Muppets.

One of my VIP spirits used to oversee the chocolate-making at Skinners. I first "met" Mary at a house party with her entire family, a sea of daughters and sons, gathered around the small, striped couch in their living room for a unique family reunion.

Mary McKenna held together this tight-knit, faith-based, Irish-Catholic family that ran Skinners. Her zest for life kept her going: to Fenway Park for a baseball game at the ripe old age of 82; wrapped in a plethora of blankets watching a Patriots football playoff game; dancing on a cruise to Bermuda; hosting parties; counseling her children and grandchildren; and diving into almost anything active, except bungee jumping. Most of her bucket-list items were checked off. An avid devotee of St. Jude and St. Jude's Hospital, she sent in a monthly donation for the kids as That Girl, Marlo Thomas, suggested. I aspire to be like Mary one day—living life to the fullest, persevering despite challenges, and loving everyone unconditionally.

I look up to Rosie this way, too—as my big sister, best friend, and mentor who lives a joyful, inspired life. She turned her bowl of lemons into a beautiful upside-down cake with extra whipped love. And like her, I intend to savor, *to live for*, every scrumptious piece of the gift called Life.

People often tell me, "You're always so positive and happy. I wish I could be more like you." I tell them, "Don't wait for someone else to bring you flowers. Plant your own garden! Spruce up your own soul!" It took plenty of work over the years to learn to be happy and positive.

What keeps us from living a fulfilled life and how do we measure what that means to us?

I believe fear is the number-one culprit keeping us prisoner in our own lives. When we step out of fear (namely, out of our comfort zone), we become more available to embrace what living life to the fullest really means.

I refuse to let fear control my decisions. I wasn't always that way. First, I had to take control of my often-unfounded fears. I took back my own power. Struggling with an anxiety disorder most of my life, I felt imprisoned by fear and low self-esteem. Panic attacks plagued me and came too often, leaving me shriveled in the corner of a room, sweating, shaking, and nauseous. I learned, slowly, to recognize my anxiety for what it really was—*just* anxiety—and how to manage it. From thereon, if I started to get all worked up, sweaty palms and all, I'd say to myself: "Okay, Maureen, this is anxiety. You know this feeling *very* well. You've done this a trillion times. You know how to handle this. This too shall pass."

I make sure to get plenty of sleep, to stay away from caffeine and sugar (well, when I can help myself, and chocolate doesn't count), and to read many inspirational books. I also learned, no matter how busy I am, to stop and take a few moments to "ground" myself. I picture myself as a tree, with both feet firmly on the ground. I envision my "roots" digging deeply into the ground, balancing my energy, and connecting me again with the earth. It's instantly calming—give it a shot some time. As I've grown in both experience and age, I've learned to quiet my mind and trust my soul by reprogramming fear-based, negative, inner messages into something more positive. In effect, I've re-recorded my life, and this time, I'm being a lot nicer to myself! I reach out to friends and family who support and love me. I trust my own path in life and accept this great gift I've been given, which was meant to be shared with others. I "pay it forward."

❧

Make a conscious effort to become aware of fear and decide not to let it weave its toxic web around you. This is the first step in awakening to the possibilities of abundant joy and laughter.

So many of my clients ask the same questions about their earthly journey: "Why am I here?" "What is the purpose of my life?" I tell them to just *live* their lives while being truly open and available to those around them. When we are open and more present for our family, relationships, work, and ourselves, what we want to accomplish with our lives becomes clearer.

Start by making goals for yourself. On a piece of paper, draw three columns. In the first column, write "Short-term Goals." In the middle column, write "Mid-term Goals," and in the third column, write "Long-term Goals." Your short-term goals should be simple, easily attainable objectives. For instance, some lighter-fare items on my short-term-goal list include: eat dinner as a family around the table, read to my children, volunteer my time, help the elderly, tip big, and smile at a stranger (but not in a psychotic, I-want-your-puppy way). My long-term goals are heftier items. One is pay off my debt and my parents' debt and purchase a compound on Martha's Vineyard where my entire family can grow old together. Another long-term goal of mine is to start a few more charities (I've already cofounded two), one of which will be a nonprofit that helps widows and widowers find love again. I want to call it "A Match Made in Heaven."

Start small and then work your way over the rainbow. And don't forget to look in the mirror. The greatest gift you've ever been given is staring right back at you. Smile.

14

Jonathan's Sunshine

I met the most awe-inspiring, remarkable, brilliant, compassionate spirit of all time a few years ago. Well, our Sean Michael is a bit more brilliant, but I know Sean proudly shares the stage with Jonathan. Jonathan's mother, Mary, came to see me at my old storefront in Middleboro. When the door chimes jingled, I came out to greet my first client of the morning.

A petite woman with a beautiful smile came toward me for a hug. She came bearing gifts. In one hand was a tape-recording machine with a bow on it, and in the other hand, a bag full of goodies—candles, chocolates, books, and flowers. I almost asked her if she was a delivery person from FTD.

"I'm giving you this recorder to use for all the parents you are help-ing with children in heaven," she said with a smile.

Mary sat down on my new chocolate-colored recliner. I sat across from her and reached out to hold her hands. I knew why she was com-ing to see me, because a friend of my sister Rosie had referred her to me.

Her son Jonathan's presence was immediate and magical. There were white sparkles of light dancing around Mary's head. I was afraid if I started the session by telling her that, she would bolt out the door. Instead, I started asking Jonathan questions in my mind to validate his presence for his mom. He talked about having been in college and what his goals for the future had been. He also mentioned an adoption.

"Jonathan is talking about a little girl. He says you are thinking of adopting her."

Mary froze. Her beautiful blue eyes widened. After a few moments, she gathered herself and spoke slowly. "There is a little girl I am helping to take care of. I've been thinking of adopting her. She's from a third-world country."

Jonathan was so excited. His energy kept surging through me like lightning. My body would jolt forward as if someone was using a defi-brillator on my chest. It wasn't scary for me at all. I was amazed at this connection. (As I'm writing this now, a white light, similar to the North Star, just appeared in front of my computer screen. I love this stuff!)

Jonathan showed me his heaven. He walked in front of me as we started to climb rolling green hills. The area was very similar to the countryside in the movie *The Sound of Music*. I felt my breath getting shorter and shorter. The colors were so brilliant. When we finally reached the top of the highest hill, there was a small schoolhouse (red—you guessed it) sitting to the left on the hill. Although the structure looked new, it had old, wooden doors on the front and a bell hanging off the front of the building.

"I'm the schoolmaster here," Jonathan told me. I teach all the children. Look out back. The children are gathered for a book reading. Every morning we take turns reading a book together."

I peaked around the building and saw a group of children giggling and hugging one another.

"Tell my mother I'm very happy. I'm helping children here just like I did there. Oh, and once in awhile I get to golf, too."

When I opened my eyes, I started to cry. I wanted Mary to experience Jonathan's heaven the way I had. I'd only lost it once before in a reading many years ago, when a young woman in spirit, Kerry, came to me just days after her passing. I am now very good friends with her sister, Kim. When I am in reading mode, I usually can't get emotionally connected to the spirit coming through—or the sitter—or I will lose the connection. With Jonathan (and Kerry), I could feel joy and elation at a higher level than with most spirits. Jonathan's heaven was so breathtaking. I really felt like I was walking with him for those few minutes.

I described every detail to Mary and tried to remember everything Jonathan relayed to me. I could see the pain lift a bit from Mary's face and her smile lit up the room.

"Tell Jonathan I'm very proud of him. He always wanted to help children. He was involved in a few charities and took great pride in giving back."

"Mary, you just told him yourself. He loved you so much and love can't possibly die."

I'd like to share with you Mary's story, told in her own words, as only a mother can do:

It was June 2001, and Jonathan was home from college. He and his two younger brothers were filled with expectations about the months ahead, and I felt the promise of a wonderful summer to come.

Jonathan's nineteenth birthday was July 3. On July 27, his vibrant life was taken from him, from us.

Jonathan was tortured and killed by a serial killer who stated, "I just wanted to kill." Three amazing people, all extremely loved, lost their lives to this evil. It was 8:00 PM on a magnificent summer night in Plymouth, Massachusetts. Countless tourists were walking the streets. Jonathan had just gotten out of work at a seaside restaurant when a monster, dressed in a business suit, carjacked and murdered our sunshine.

In one moment our lives were shattered and forever changed. All my beliefs were thrown into the air and tossed around. Nothing made any sense. Jonathan was not found for four days. It was the longest four days of our lives—agonizing days for family and friends, search teams, police, the FBI, detectives, psychics . . . and then they found our beautiful son. I begged to go to him, to give him my love, but because it was a crime scene, and later, because everyone thought it was best that I didn't, I never sent my son off with a hug. Every day of their lives, my boys hugged me numerous times, knowing it was the best present they could ever give me. I live with the regret that I wasn't stronger or more insistent about giving Jonathan a last hug—every mother has the right to hug her child.

Some believed that the trial and justice would bring us "closure." Such an absurd word and thought, as there will be no closure until we are together again. Some days, in the darkest of holes, this is all I wanted. Gradually, slower than you can possibly imagine, I knew I had to live, and my two youngest boys deserved the mom and the life of joy they once had.

I did not care about myself. I loved my husband and my boys with all my heart, but that was all I was capable of. Even their sports games seemed violent to me. Our privacy was gone, and I felt as if everyone was staring at me. Sometimes people thought it would help to offer their opinions on the ways this killer should die.

I couldn't stand it and often became a hermit in our house. Gratefully, those who had no words just hugged me tight. I was not filled with anger as many thought I should be. I had no room in my body for it; my body was overflowing with sadness and confusion. I would write daily in a journal to Jonathan, and filled ten books with pages that just said, "Come home, Jonathan." "Why?" "I miss you, sunshine." And "I love you."

I knew in my heart and soul Jonathan would somehow let me know he was still around. His energy and love were too strong not to come through. And I also knew he would expect me to try everything that might help me believe in and feel his love.

The hugs and kindness of family, friends, my homicide counselor, and even strangers, saved my life. Yet my spirit felt so dark and heavy, my body physically hurt, and my mind relived every detail of Jonathan's fear and death. Grief is a long and lonely road but one that must be walked or crawled. I tried staying busy, even painted every room a different color for weeks on end. I tried pretending Jonathan was back at college. I felt crazy and anxious, and always, the sadness would catch up with me and I would crumble.

The first year graces you with numbness and shock. The second year is harder as you realize you have to go through another year of missing your child. But the third year, for me, was the worst. Everyone seemed to be healing and carrying on, but I struggled every single day to get out of the darkness. Maybe it was the impending trial of Jonathan's killer—I don't know—but I hit rock bottom. My heart, mind, and body felt broken and irreparable.

Thankfully, I would picture the sweet faces of my boys, knowing I couldn't cause them anymore pain, and I would crawl back out my darkness again and again, until I finally felt it was time to find a way to live with this pain.

I began searching for the meaning of life. Why was such an old soul like Jonathan, who believed in the ripple effect of kindness, taken— when all who knew him believed he would have continued to do great things? I prayed and begged for the nightmares to end and to have a dream of Jonathan instead.

I read hundreds of books: religious, spiritual, historical— everything—looking for answers, but none came. No book tells your story or can begin to capture the love and loss of your own child.

What I did gain from these books was the knowledge that for many, many generations, people have survived immeasurable loss. For those who didn't, it was their choice.

I didn't want to live in despair. I desperately wanted to hold onto my belief that there is an abundance of goodness and kindness in this world, and most of all, I feared my boys would grow up to be bitter and angry, instead of loving and giving. I wanted to find a way to love my life again.

I started doing things I never would have imagined doing before, just to get through the days. I had my tarot cards read by many and traveled all over to different psychics and mediums, always filled with hope but never feeling a true connection to Jonathan.

The day I stepped into Maureen's small building, I felt a calmness I couldn't explain, a sense of peace that had been lacking for so long. The minute she stepped out of her office, the room filled with her enormous energy and love. She immediately started talking passionately, using her arms and hands, unable to control her emotions, with the same enthusiasm that Jonathan once had. I knew without a doubt in those first few minutes that Jonathan was trying to talk to me through Maureen.

She told me many things that validated my belief, things no one could have ever known. But it was this comment that made me a true believer: "Jonathan wants you to remember and think about the conversation you had with him a few days before he died." I had not shared this conversation with anyone. Only Jonathan and I were present.

I had told him that he was working too much and I missed him. He laughed and said, "Mom, you're the best. Most moms tell their kids to work more. You tell us you miss us and to work less!" So, he took the day off and we went to his favorite Italian restaurant and talked for hours, enjoying each other's company as we always did. I told him I felt a deep sense of dread and panic and had had a terrible nightmare the night before in which one of my boys died. I said it couldn't have been him because I kept telling him he couldn't go back to college. I even asked him not to share this with Nick and Elliot as I didn't want to scare them. (I had never had such a nightmare. My nights were once filled with amazing, belly-laughing dreams.) Tears flowed from my eyes as I shared my fear with him.

"I wouldn't survive. I wouldn't be able to go on if one of my boys died. You and your brothers are my life." He looked at me with those brilliant blue eyes and said, "Mom, I don't know where this is coming from, but first of all, you are much stronger than you think. You taught us to make the best of our days, to give to others, to be kind to everyone. And we both have shared our belief that our time is determined and not in our control. We just have to live each day with great enthusiasm and make a difference in this world."

A chill went through my entire body, and Jonathan asked if I wanted my sweater. I remember his concerned eyes and told him, "No, just hug me tight."

I look back on this day now and realize what a gift it was—one of many gifts given to me from our son. It was Maureen who reminded me of them and I will forever be grateful. She also asked me, "What does 'last hug' mean? Jonathan is telling me there *is* no last hug."

Something suddenly became clear—after all those weeks and years of wishing I had and regretting I didn't hug him in death: there is no last hug. We will hug again. The circle that began the moment he was placed on my heart at birth will continue until we meet again.

I don't believe in coincidences anymore. People cross our paths for a reason. I have met the most amazing people of courage and grace in the past years. I have been inspired by many. I also know now that we have a choice in how we want to walk with the pain of missing our children every single day. Many people (who generally mean well) repeatedly tell me that Jonathan would not want me to be sad. I always reply, "Jonathan would understand my pain and knows I need to grieve in my own time." If my words convey anything to you, I sincerely pray I have given you a little hope. Our hearts are graced with hope and the desire to laugh, love, and give to others despite our journeys. Jonathan is with me, his love has no boundaries, and I believe he understands his life path, something we will never comprehend while we remain here.

Eventually everything will make sense and all the whys will be answered. I once thought that when Jonathan died, a huge part of my heart went with him in death, but I now know he left a piece of his heart with me instead. He has given me a strength I never thought possible. I am not afraid of death and I will not go before my time. I am here to honor and cherish love. I feel intense gratitude that at least we had Jonathan in our life. All the pain is worth the genuine love he gave and continues to give us. He was a gift in this life and I believe he is continuing on his new path, helping and loving with even greater magnitude. Try to just remember the love. Nothing else matters or is as comforting as the love of a child.

The unimaginable happened to Mary's family—her son was murdered. Although she grieves every day, she has found a way to be present for her family and to honor Jonathan's memory with love. I gain great strength from Mary—she is the epitome of triumph over tragedy.

As a lasting memory of his life and in support of the charities that he championed, Jonathan's parents, Mary and Mike Rizzo, established the Jonathan Rizzo Memorial Foundation in 2001 (www.jonathan rizzofoundation.org).

The foundation is unique in its support for a gamut of worthy causes. In lieu of raising money to fund a specific cause, it targets the giving where it is needed most and can do the most good. The generosity of many has funded everything from heat in the winter for a cancer-stricken mother of two to private high-school education for teenagers of a family that lost their father to a new soccer field for kids in Massachusetts, and most recently, refugee children in Rwanda, Africa. The foundation also provides support for charities that were important to Jonathan, including Christmas in the City and the Sleeping Children Across the World Foundation.

Through the foundation, Jonathan's spirit continues on, doing the kind of things he did during his all-too-short nineteen years and reminding all of us that it is not how long we are here that counts but what we do while we're here. As the anthropologist Margaret Mead once said, "Never doubt that a small group of thoughtful, committed citizens can change the world. Indeed, it is the only thing that ever has."

ᘒ

Be patient with yourself and those around you, especially your children. Each day is a gift and should be cherished.

The attitude you choose each morning will determine how the rest of your day plays out. How will you make the best of your days? Keep it simple. Make a conscious effort to be more positive. Understand that every challenge you face is an opportunity for growth. Give back in small ways that make you feel good inside. There is a light at the end of the tunnel. Remember, the seed of hope was planted at birth—it's up to you to nourish it.

15

Surviving for Bo

It was two days before Christmas and I was running around frantically trying to finish my shopping. I'm "last-minute Lucy," running around the mall overspending, buying elaborate gifts like the Shiatsu Full-Body Massager at Brookstone, the "feels like a real man is pummeling you" gift that will get used once on Christmas morning. Holiday music echoes from the rooftop, grating on my nerves like a badly played version of Aerosmith's "Dude Looks Like a Lady," on *Guitar Hero*.

My thoughts drifted to the parent-support-group appearance I'd be making later that evening at my office for those who have lost a child. As I watched the droves of miserable people scowling and fighting with cashiers about sale items and returns, I thought about my special guests—here on earth and there in heaven—who I'd see that night. I wanted to shout from the top of the escalator, "Do you have any clue how lucky and blessed you all are?! You're buying presents, hopefully in a way that expresses your love, for a *living* person. Most of the parents I help refuse to put up a tree or light candles. It takes all the energy they can muster just to survive the holidays."

As I left the mall, George Foreman grill in tow, I turned on the radio and prepared for the support-group meeting. Every song that came on seemed to speak to me from the "kids" in heaven. Between the voices and the goose bumps on the back of my neck, the energy in my car was palpable. One smart-aleck spirit threw something from my messy backseat. I believe it was a spitball. These kids in heaven are playful, mischievous, and excited to be hanging with "Moprah" (that's me).

When I pulled into the parking lot of my office, the lot was full. I wondered if maybe there was a last-minute run on manicures/pedicures at the Asian nail shop at the end of my office building.

Climbing the stairs to the workshop room for the group meeting, I felt dizzy. I leaned against the wall and sat on the fifth stair. *Whew, what did I get myself into?* I thought. *Connecting to one or two young people is hard enough, never mind a whole roomful. Help me, angels. Help me, God.*

Sixty people filled the room. I was surprised by the laughter and lively conversation. My sister Rosie, who facilitates the group, sat at the front, overlooking the crowd. I tried to slip in inconspicuously and hide in the corner.

I was standing at the front of the room when I saw a woman coming through the door. Her husband was holding her up as she leaned into him sobbing. She was in a trancelike state. I could see her husband squeeze her hand tightly; he was crying, too. They both looked at me with such sadness in their eyes, and I knew they were eagerly waiting to hear from their precious son.

I leaned over and asked the woman her name. In a barely audible whisper she said, "Suzie." After she took her seat I knelt before her. I took her hands in mine. A gush of warmth spread through my body. I smiled at Suzie and said, "Bo is where he is supposed to be. He'd just been going up and down for so long. He finally has peace."

I touched her neck and told her that her son had passed by hanging. Suzie nodded her head, barely able to take a breath.

"He's telling me that he's the baby," I said.

She replied, "He's not. That's not true."

"He is insisting that he is the baby of the first three, and then you had three others. There are six altogether," I replied.

Suzie looked at her husband and started laughing. She said, "I had three children when we first met and Bo was the baby at the time. Anthony and I then had three more together."

Suzie told me she could feel herself getting lighter, and she truly knew that Bo was connecting with me.

I've connected thousands of children with their parents over the years, but this reading was exceptional. Bo went on to give so many validations to his parents to help them heal.

I was standing in front of his dad when I heard in my head, "He's 'Big A' for Anthony." I shared this with Bo's dad and he chuckled.

"Bo says that you didn't like his new tattoo, but you love it now." Suzie said she and Anthony hated the tattoo Bo had on his arm. But it wasn't until after he passed that they learned what the Latin words, *Vive Doe et Vies*, written under his cross tattoo meant: "Live for God, and You Shall Have Life."

Then I looked directly at Anthony, "You weren't happy about coming here tonight, but he's so glad that you did. He helped you get here, actually."

Suzie blurted out, "We thought we wouldn't make it. We were completely stopped in traffic. Then, it just opened up and we made it here with a minute left to spare."

"He's telling me he tried to take his life once before," I said.

Suzie had a puzzled look on her face as if she was confused.

"No," Suzie told me.

"He's insisting he did," I replied.

Suzie looked at me and said, "This is shocking. I am suddenly remembering what I saw a few weeks before Bo died—blue marks on his neck. I asked him what happened and he gave me some story. I asked if he tried to hurt himself. He hesitated, looked up to the sky, and said, "No." If only I had understood what that hesitation meant. We found out later that he told some of his friends what he tried to do. He also told his friends that I knew and was getting him help—so no one saw the need to tell me."

I held Suzie's hands and said, "Bo wants me to do this to you."

I picked her up and spun her around. After I put her down, Suzie grinned from ear to ear and said, "Bo used to pick me up and spin me around when I visited him at work—we'd spin until we were dizzy. I used to yell at him because I thought we were going to fall."

After the meeting, I approached Suzie and Anthony. I offered to give them a private reading, at no cost, in the near future. I told them I rarely feel such a strong spirit as I had felt Bo, especially since he had so recently crossed over. Bo just wouldn't shut up and was trying to dominate the entire evening.

"You know, your son has absolutely no spirit etiquette," I said laughing.

The next morning, Suzie called to make their private appointment. She said she crossed her fingers that the wait wouldn't be too long. Her finger-crossing worked, because exactly two months later, they got their appointment. Suzie and Anthony said they counted the days until our meeting.

Suzie told me after that meeting: "I keep replaying everything you said to us at that support-group session. And that was only in about ten minutes! This time, we'd get a whole hour with you. This is what kept me sane and optimistic. Anthony and I had finally found some peace at the group. You changed our lives forever."

February 16, 2008

Suzie and Anthony's appointment was at 11:00 AM. I told them to bring a tape recorder, if they wanted. They showed up with a small recorder they borrowed from a friend. I looked through the glass partition separating my office from the reception area. I could see two young girls with them. The girls did not look happy to be there—both had their arms folded and one had a scowl on her face. I quickly took off my jacket and burst into the room.

"Bo hid my keys and bothered me the whole car ride to the office!" I exclaimed. The young girls looked at each other and rolled their eyes.

"Turn on your recorder," I told Suzie. "He's ready to go."

"Who's Carly? Bo was repeating that name to me the whole time in the car," I asked.

The girl to the right of me squirmed in her chair.

"I am," she said hesitantly.

"Bo's telling me about the i-Pod in your room, how it randomly goes off at about 2:00 AM, waking you and your roommate up," I said.

Carly's eyes lit up. "That happens every night!" she squealed. She beamed with pride. I felt like she was warming up to me and the possibility of life after death.

Next, I turned to face Bo's other sister.

"Bo's telling me you have a little son, whom he loves very much. He's telling me about the time your son lost a tooth in an accident when he was about two years old."

"Oh my God! My son, Cameron, fell on the sidewalk when he was two and lost a front tooth."

"Your brother also wants me to remind you that he's always with you. You know those crazy noises in your apartment, how things literally fly off the shelves sometimes? Bo's telling me that's his way of trying to get your attention. He doesn't want to freak you out, he just wants to tell you he's there with you. He loves you so very much."

Bo's sister sat there with her head in her hands, sobbing. I reached over and took her hands in mine.

"Who is Chris and what's the "L" name connection?" I asked.

"Chris is my fiancé, and my name is Lauren." She replied.

"Well, Bo wants him to get a tattoo of his name right next to his freckle."

Lauren and Carly covered their mouths, screamed, and then started laughing hysterically.

"Chris has a mole on his cheek that Bo used to tease him about, calling it a 'freckle.' Chris hated being teased about his freckle."

As I talked with Lauren and Carly about all sorts of things in their lives, they were so enthralled, and all their skepticism vanished.

Now, it was Anthony's turn.

"Bo's telling me about the flight school you sent him to in Florida, and how much he loved it. He's also asking me to tell you that now he knows he should have listened to you more." I held Anthony's hands tightly and said, "Bo is so grateful for how much you helped him, even though he didn't give you too much credit while he was alive. Bo wants to say he's sorry for that. He's thanking you for trying everything with him, and he wants me to tell you he's always loved you very much—now he just understands you better."

Anthony's eyes filled up and he smiled.

"Oh, and there's one more thing," I said. "Bo wants to thank you for giving him a silver cross at his high-school graduation that your grandmother gave you from Italy. Bo is saying thank you for putting that in the casket, because he knew it meant a lot to you."

Suzie started crying. She said she remembered the day of Bo's wake when Anthony suddenly remembered the cross hanging on their bedpost for fifteen years. Anthony asked her to wash it and put it on Bo.

Suzie was fidgeting and I could see she was getting antsy. Finally, I swung my chair over to her, and held my hands out to her. Suzie started to frantically tell me about all the signs that they had received over the last two months.

"I had a dream of Bo, and I just know it wasn't an ordinary dream; it was a real 'visit.' In the dream, he hugged me, and looked directly in my eyes and said, 'Mom, my numbers are 2, 6, 11, and sometimes 26—I love you. Then, the next day I was telling my nephew about the dream. Suddenly my sister's phone beeped with a new text message. My sister had no idea about my dream and innocently held up her phone blurting out, 'Look! This is the third time I got this text! The first one read 261126112611, the second one read 112611261126, and the third one read 621162116211!' My nephew and I fell to our knees screaming, while the rest of the family thought we were nuts. That's really Bo doing all these things, isn't it Maureen?"

I looked at Suzie and smiled.

"Bo is not dead; he is just different," I stated.

As they got up to leave, we all hugged and Suzie said to me, "Thank you and Bo for being the greatest teachers we've ever had. We can survive this nightmare now."

Once in awhile a spirit will amaze me with its capability to reach its family after such a short time out of its physical body. In Bo's case, he struggled so much before his passing— he needed his family to know that he was finally at peace. Like many families going through a similar challenge, Bo's family tried to help him, but couldn't fix him. Although Suzie and Anthony were what I call "healthy skeptics," they gave spirit communication a chance, and that little seed of hope has blossomed and will continue to flower around them for years to come.

I've met thousands of people over the years in this work, from all walks of life. Some were believers, some were healthy skeptics, and others didn't have one belief left, after experiencing some of the most trying times of their lives in the physical loss of loved ones. I've been there, too, when you just don't think you can hold out hope any longer, when the trials and tribulations simply seem too long, or too heavy. Yet, it is in these precise moments, that hope truly does exist. After all, hope floats—always. Even when we can't "see it"—in fact, especially when we can't see it—it is there. There is a huge shift in consciousness taking place at this moment in time. Millions are reaching out for some sort of validation that they are not alone. We all get signs whether we acknowledge them or not. As humans, we try to rationalize what we are experiencing and talk ourselves out of a beautiful gift from beyond. Trust your heart and listen in a new way: open to the possibilities, open to hope, and open to the continuation of your passed one's love, which they are trying to show you. It's always there, right along with your loved ones in spirit, holding you up and filling you with a new way of thinking and renewed hope.

16

Expect the Unexpected

I was doing a demonstration at Uplifting Connections, a wellness center and bookstore five minutes from my home. I love the energy in this quaint, special gathering space. The owner, my friend Ellie, found a way to give back to the community and nurture her own spiritual growth after her husband passed from a brain tumor. The walls are painted burnt orange with ornamental stars lit up and hung around the perimeter of the store. There are shelves of classy, unique gifts and books spread around the space. For my gatherings, fifty chairs are squeezed into the middle of the store. At the beginning of this event, I immediately noticed a woman sitting in the last row, under a cluster stars. Her mother in spirit was pushing me to approach her.

"I have your mom in spirit here. Did she pass from lung cancer?"

"Oh my God, yes. She was sick for two months."

"She's showing me a scene of you trying to fix her hair in the coffin. She said they did an awful job, and she didn't wear her hair like that."

The daughter gasped loudly and her face flushed. "My mother was always perfectly coiffed," she explained to me. "I said to my sister, Diane, that Mom would be mortified if anyone saw her hair. When nobody was looking, we took turns trying to fix it. She looked like Phyllis Diller after a night of partying."

I could hear huffing and puffing coming from her mother—I guess she wasn't too thrilled with the Phyllis Diller reference. She asked me to thank her daughter for at least trying to fix her hair.

After a physical passing, a spirit will hang around for a few days to make sure everyone is okay and to oversee the services. At this recent event, the mom came through to let her daughter know she also wasn't thrilled with how the undertaker had prepared her for the services. Normally, spirits are no longer attached to how they physically look, but on occasion, if a woman was particular about her appearance here, it may carry over for a short time there.

Thousands of people come to me after the loss of a loved one has left them paralyzed by grief. Many want a sign or direct connection to help them know their loved one in spirit is okay and at peace. I tell everyone that we are all mediums. I just happen to trust what I hear, see, and feel, which gives me confidence that I am truly bridging the gap between this world and the next. Just like an instrument, if I fine-tune my gift by using it daily, the output is a beautifully orchestrated flow of information.

There are many stages to the grieving process but everyone grieves differently. My friend Marianne, whose amazing son, Jesse, passed five years ago, informed me about a recent proposed fifth edition of the *Diagnostic and Statistical Manual of Mental Disorders* by the American Psychiatric Association. The proposal suggests that if you have lost a loved one, you have two weeks to grieve before they diagnose you with clinical depression. So, if you've lost a child or close relative and, after two weeks, you're still feeling sad, uninterested in things, can't sleep, or don't want to go to work, according to the manual, you have major depression and need drugs. Who writes this stuff? Drug-company executives?

I believe many people benefit from medication to help with depression and other challenges. However, if this new guideline is adopted, many people who experience completely normal grief could be mislabeled as having a psychiatric problem. Even the current manual proposes an unrealistic standard of two months of grieving before one is considered clinically depressed. I don't think the answer for most grieving people is a diagnosis such as this and a prescription for pills— sometimes for life. Reach out to a grief counselor and discuss other options to help you sleep and get through the day, but don't fall for the pharmaceutical companies' take on grief.

They say time heals all wounds. Grief is a different story. The hole in your heart will always be there, but over time you learn to fill it with little pieces of joy. I call it "heart spackle." You will have good days and bad days. Sometimes the spackle will crack and you have to find new ways to get through the day. Reach out to a friend you can trust who can help pull you out of bed.

After my nephew, Sean, passed, my sister was understandably mad at God. She put up her dukes and took him on. She screamed her heart and soul out to him: "How could you do this?! How could you take my baby?!" In the support group she facilitates for parents who have lost children, she talks about her struggle to understand how God could do this to our family. Rosie is a tough cookie, so God was smart to just listen.

Eventually, we all began to accept that Sean was meant to be in his physical incarnation for nineteen years. Sean came to me in a dream and told me this. I looked at the clock and it was just after midnight. I just finished a large event and was exhausted. When my head hit the pillow I started to drift off to sleep. I was walking along the beach in what appeared to be the Caribbean. The water was turquoise and the sand was almost white. Coming toward me was our Sean! He was smiling and ran to hug me. While he was holding me tight I asked him if he was okay. He spoke directly into my ear and said, "Auntie Moey, my soul agreement for this lifetime was nineteen years. That's how long I was scheduled to be here." I felt a light, warm wind brush against my face and then I awoke. He touched more lives in his short physical time here than most people do over many years.

Your true friends reveal themselves in the days and weeks after a loss. The house is filled with relatives and friends after the services. Children shriek and run through the rooms of the house, unaware of the deep sadness that hides behind the walls. Laughter echoes from the kitchen as stories are shared of the *missing* special guest: *Remember when Dad used to take his teeth out and chase the kids around the yard, flapping them open and shut. I bet he's chuckling right now looking down on us.*

For a few days after a funeral, the calls and visits are plentiful. Then, about a week after, when the dust settles, it's like a ghost town in the home. Some people just can't handle death. They run from it. It makes them uncomfortable to see a person in pain and crying. I think it makes them look at their own lives and family. We run from any intimations of our mortality.

Spirit signs are plentiful in the beginning. Spirits often use their newfound energy to manipulate electricity or anything mechanical. Lights may flicker or blow out; the phone may ring and nobody will be there; televisions turn on and off; musical toys randomly play; and alarm clocks ring. These signs will come when you least expect them, so watch and listen for them, and expect the unexpected.

In the early stages after a passing, the spirit is trying to adjust to their new spirit body. The time it takes an individual spirit to get used to this is different for each spirit. They might show up in a dream or you may see a shadow walk by in a hallway—not in a creepy *Nightmare on Elm Street* way, but just to let you know they're still around.

In one of my sessions, a woman recalled how her mother appeared to her a week after her physical death. This woman was upstairs cleaning and heard someone at the door.

I heard the doorbell ring. I went downstairs and before I hit the bottom step, I felt a flutter in my chest. I imagined opening the door and seeing my mother standing there smiling. I called out asking who was there and got no reply. My heart was pounding. I opened the door and there she was, smiling from ear to ear. She looked so young—how I remember her from years ago. Her skin was clear and glowing, with no wrinkles. Her hair was styled the way she wore it in her forties.

I couldn't believe my eyes. My human brain took over and I couldn't stop asking her how she was able to be there. She said, "Aren't you going to ask me in for coffee?" We always met for coffee. It was our thing. She said, "I can't stay long. I just need you to know I am fine. It may seem like I'm not here with you anymore, but I most certainly am. Tell your sister I stopped by."

We laughed until we cried, just like the old days. I could smell her Jean Naté body splash. We hugged and I held her tight, inhaling her essence. She turned around and walked over to the door. Before walking out, she smiled and waved. "You'll be fine," she said.

One of the most amazing ways I've ever seen spirit connect is through an electronic voice phenomenon (EVP). EVP is a mysterious event in which human-sounding voices from an unknown source are heard on audiotape, in radio station noise, and through other electronic media. Most often, EVPs have been captured on audiotape. The mysterious voices are not heard at the time of the original recording; the voices appear only when the tape is played back. Sometimes amplification and noise filtering are required to hear the voices. Some EVPs are more easily heard and understood than others. And they vary in gender (men and women), age (adults and children), tone, and emotion. EVP voices usually speak in single words, phrases, or short sentences. Sometimes they just grunt, groan, growl, or make other vocal sounds. EVPs have been recorded speaking in various languages. I have personally heard EVPs recorded in my private sessions only a few times.

My friend Eric Lavoie, a paranormal investigator, has played EVPs for me from a few of his investigations. I have to be honest—sometimes they are a little creepy. Eric and I did a quick measuring of spirit energy at the historic Middleboro, Massachusetts, town hall. When we were walking up the stairway that led to the balcony of the Great Hall, I felt a chill travel up my back. When we got to the top stair, Eric played back the tape he was recording on, and we were both stunned to hear what sounded like several women laughing. It was crystal clear. Needless to say, I quickly scooted back down the stairs and out the door. Even though I do what I do, there are times my work surprises and stuns me.

One very special spirit friend I've met along my journey who helps me every day is Nicky O'Neill. On February 20, 2003, eighteen-year-old Nicholas O'Neill passed away in the fourth deadliest nightclub fire in United States history. The Station nightclub in West Warwick, Rhode Island, was totally engulfed in flames in just ten seconds because of a combination of indoor pyrotechnics and flammable soundproofing insulation. An old friend of mine, Carla Bagtaz, also passed in the fire.

Nick was an actor, musician, comedian, composer, and writer. When he was just sixteen, Nick wrote a one-act play called *They Walk Among Us*. This play is about teenagers who die and return as guardian angels. His dad says this work is not only prophetic but a moving and inspirational celebration of life and hope.

Since Nick's passing, his family and friends have experienced a myriad of unexplained signs and events, most of these connected with the number 41. His parents, Dave and Joanne, came to see me not long after Nicky's passing. When I greeted them at the door of my old storefront, they smiled warmly, yet seemed a little anxious. I had no idea who they were hoping to hear from as they made there way to my treatment room in the back of the store. I brought in a chair and placed it next to the recliner. Enya was echoing in the background accompanied by the sound of water trickling out of a bamboo fountain.

After explaining how I connect to spirit, I immediately felt the energy of a younger male. He was telling me he passed tragically. I had a hard time interpreting symbols that I later realized were for a fire. I also saw a scene playing out in my head of a male passing by impact in a car accident. Nick's parents confirmed that Nick's friend, Eric, passed before him in a car accident. I felt a connection to Nick similar to the one I had with my nephew, Sean.

Suddenly, as energy surged through me, I felt the urge to get up and jump around the room like Mick Jagger. I was doing impressions and dancing like Michael Jackson. Halfway through the session I needed a nap. This spirit had more energy than Jim Carrey in *The Mask*. As Nick was coming through, it was like he took over my body. He wanted to make his parents smile and remember what a character he was in his physical body. Nick was a very expressive and animated young man, and spoke through me: "Tell my dad his mother is here. Bring up the name Bill. He's here, too. My mother will know what I'm talking about. Tell them I have my black guitar. I love music. Bring up the name Chris. Say hi to my brothers."

Nick went on and on, giving validations and making his parents laugh. Nick and I bonded that day.

During the session, I kept asking Nicky's mom, "Can't you hear him? He keeps saying he's calling out to you." She insisted she couldn't hear him. When she got home and listened to the tape I recorded in our session, she heard a strange voice come over the recording—an EVP:

Me: "Can't you hear him? He keeps saying he's calling out to you."

Joanne: "No, I don't hear him. I don't know what he's talking about."

EVP: "Mommy."

Later that month, Joanne played the tape back for me. Everyone who listens to it can hear Nick calling out to his mother. Dave and Joanne contacted a specialist on EVPs who lived out West. Margaret has special equipment that can pick up subtle EVPs as she connects to the spirit. During her recorded session with the O'Neills, the following EVP was picked up:

"Hey, Mom, it's me, Nick."

I listened to the actual recording and got goose bumps. Joanne said the EVP came through in Nick's voice.

The O'Neills told another client of mine about their experience with EVPs. Suzie, Bo's mom from Chapter 15, contacted Margaret to see if her son would be able to come through with his own EVP.

Suzie wrote to Margaret and told her about Bo. A couple of weeks later, she received an e-mail from Margaret informing her that she thought she had received an EVP from Bo the night before, and she wanted Suzie to confirm the voice.

Suzie was just getting ready for mass on a Sunday morning. When she opened the e-mail and clicked on the EVP link, she heard the following: "Hey, Mom, it's me, Bo." She then clicked on the next link. Margaret was doing the talking.

"Who is this? Who am I talking with?"

"It's me, Bo. I'm talking, talking to Mom!" He was loud and sounded frustrated with Margaret for not knowing who he was. Suzie was crying and laughing, completely overwhelmed by what she was hearing—it could not have sounded more like Bo.

The only other time I experienced an EVP in one of my own sessions is when I met with a woman named Eileen. When Eileen climbed the stairs to my new office, she was tired and out of breath. Her face looked drained and pale. She was sweating profusely. When she sat down, she immediately began to weep. I consoled her and started to make the connection with her mother.

"Your mother is here. She is showing me she passed from congestive heart failure. Are you one of three? She is bringing up the number three. She wants to lift you up by your bootstraps and help you out of this depression."

Later that night, after the reading with Eileen, I was at my office listening to messages on my machine. I could barely make out the first message. A voice was shrieking and panting on the line. It's been years since I made or received a prank phone call, but this sure did sound like one.

After the third play, I barely could make out the voice, but I got a name and used caller ID for the number to return the call.

"Maureen, it's me, Eileen. I played the tape back today from our session, and I want you to hear something."

Eileen was giddy with excitement. I could hear her in the background rushing around to get the cassette recorder set up. Here's what she played for me over the phone:

Me: "She wants to lift you up by your bootstraps and help you out of this depression."

EVP: "Smile, smile."

"Maureen, could you hear that? That was my mother's voice! I can't get over this. I've been playing it over and over. I'm going to send you a copy. I know this is my mother's way of helping me get out of my depression. I will forever be thankful to you and her for this gift."

Even though I have the ability to connect with spirit, there are still some things that completely baffle me or leave me with questions.

After meeting Nick O'Neill, I see the number 41 everywhere, and my abilities have increased tenfold. Just by reading this, you too will be hit with the 41 bug—get ready! You will see it on many things, including shampoo, milk cartons, license plates, table numbers, billboards, mayonnaise, electronic equipment, and clothing. Nick's dad, Dave Kane, wrote a book called *41 Signs of Hope*, which chronicles his family's unexplained signs and experiences connected with the number 41. Additionally, Nick's brother, Chris O'Neill, and his friend Christian DeRezendes, directed and produced the documentary film *41*.

Whenever parents come in to connect with their children, there's Nick in my mind's eye, smiling and ready for action. I ask Nick and

Sean to help me before every show. I also ask a special angel, Jennifer Fay (a girl from Brockton, Massachusetts, who has been missing since November 1989) to assist. The three musketeers come running before I start any reading, event, or class.

I was doing a demonstration at Raffael's, a midsize restaurant in Hull, Massachusetts. The restaurant is inside the Clarion Hotel, which sits on historic Nantasket Beach, next to one of the oldest carousels in the world.

On my way to the event, Nick showed up and whispered in my ear. He told me that at the show that night would be a woman whose son had passed in a car accident and that I would know who the woman was by the number 41.

I parked my car across the street on the ocean side. The wind swept my hair in front of my face. I heard the people parked next to me giggling. I'm quite certain it was because I looked just like Cousin It from *The Addams Family*. The sound of the ocean melted the tension I felt. I knew Nick was working overtime to help this young man reunite with his mother.

When I took the stage, my eyes scanned the room looking for the number 41. I checked table numbers, T-shirts, pins, hats, and tattoos. . . nothing. The room was L-shaped. I walked around the corner to the other half of the "L" and something caught my eye. Through the stunning floor-to-ceiling glass windows, I found my 41. Parked almost to the glass of the window was a car with the numbers 141 on the license plate. A woman's head blocked the rest of the numbers on the plate. I could hear a young man screaming in my head with such excitement.

"That's my mother. The one with the big head and eighties hairdo!"

I've never been more sure of a connection in my experiences with the deceased.

"Your son is passed," I stated. "He hit a tree in a car accident. I'm hearing the name Mike."

The look on this woman's face was priceless. She is part of the reason why I continue to do this work. "Oh my God, yes! I can't believe this is happening. My Michael. Is he okay?"

"He's more than okay. He wants you to know he was with you when you found out. There was a delay in being notified. They couldn't find you."

"You're absolutely right. I was in New Hampshire and the police couldn't find me. I wasn't notified until three hours later. I'm still angry at myself for not being there for my son when he needed me most."

"Please let go of that unwanted anger," I said. "Since they couldn't find you, he came to be with you in spirit. He's happy because he knows you will be together again one day. For now, live for him, breathe him in, feel his presence, and trust he is your angel."

When she moved her hair, I could see the rest of the license plate: XO-141. Nick O'Neill had just sent me a hug and a kiss from heaven. I am so blessed.

❧

The ongoing connection we allow ourselves to feel with our spirit loved ones can help us to not only survive our deepest sorrow, suffering, and pain, but also experience triumph over tragedy. Losing someone or something we love can remind us not only how fragile and temporary life is, but also how important it is to appreciate all of the many blessings in our life: family, friends, good health, and so on.

In addition to the many signs that start to trickle down from the heavens after loss, there are many ways to commemorate and celebrate our loved ones' memory. Here are some ideas to help you get started: start a scholarship fund in your loved one's name; plan a gathering on a birthday or anniversary of your deceased loved one and let a balloon go. Children may benefit by writing a note and attaching it to the balloon; plant a memory garden with some of your loved one's favorite flowers; plant a tree in the backyard; make a CD with their favorite songs; have a pillow made out of your spirit loved one's favorite shirt or jacket; have bracelets or necklaces made out of flowers from their services; organize and create a scrapbook with pictures and items that make you smile; and, write letters to your loved one in a journal and document signs that you receive.

Although the feelings that accompany grief and the mourning process can be painful and at times exhausting, one does not "get over" grief. It's important for those grieving to learn to integrate loss into their lives so that it becomes a part of them, not what defines them. Grief is a never-ending process, but feelings change over time and many people report that, in time, they are able to live life and enjoy life. They learn to live a life that is a "new normal" and accept that there is no going back to the life they lived before the physical loss.

So many people grieve in silence or are torn apart by grief. Although it's reassuring to hear from a spirit loved one through a medium, it can be addicting. Mediumship is just one tool on your road to healing and recovery. I recommend seeking the help of a professional grief counselor to give you weekly support and guidance through the grieving process. Grief support groups may also be available in your area. Please don't hesitate to reach out for help. If you are interested in seeking out a medium, be aware that there are spirit mediums who are not coming from the heart and will take advantage of those who are grieving. Make sure you get a referral to a reputable medium.

17

Tales from the
Trenches

Over the years, I've had close encounters with people from all walks of life: celebrities, professional athletes, police officers, firemen, nurses, doctors, blue- and white-collar workers, octogenarians, mothers, fathers, and even a dog. I want to share with you some of the most touching, awe-inspiring, laugh-out-loud tales from the trenches of the "Comedian Medium." I bring through spirits in a unique way and raise the energy in a room through laughter. Our loved ones in spirit want to celebrate the good memories—not relive another wake.

One of my favorite memories stems from an event I did at the Fireside Restaurant. As I approached one of the tables, I could see the nervous excitement on an older woman's face. Her cheeks turned a rosy pink, and she squirmed around in her chair. I said, "Ma'am, is your husband passed?" It was as if I shouted, "You're the next contestant on *The Price Is Right*." She leapt out of her chair, knocking it over as she shuffled toward me, frantically tuning her hearing aids.

"Yes, Maureen, my husband's dead," she said matter-of-factly.

I felt a sharp pain in my liver and pancreas area, indicating the spirit was trying to tell me how he passed.

"He's showing me he had cancer."

She nodded yes.

"Pancreatic?"

Her eyes grew wider as she tilted her head back and grabbed the microphone right out of my hand.

"Patriotic, of course he was patriotic! He was born on the Fourth of July!"

The audience rose to their feet in a thundering applause.

Several years ago, when I first started doing private readings, an older woman in her eighties walked into my storefront on a rainy Monday. Clothed in a short dungaree skirt, leggings, and a brown polka-dot bandana around her neck, she was dressed younger than her years. I imagined this is what an elderly Dolly Parton would look like. She asked if I had any time to do a short reading.

I liked her spunk so I agreed to squeeze her in. We sat in the front of the store on the old antique couch my mother gave me. I asked my special guest her name and she replied, "You tell me." I've heard that a million times, but I did laugh out loud. Guess what her name was? Dolly!

I began the session holding her hands and closing my eyes to connect. In my head, I asked for loved ones in spirit to step forward if they wanted to talk to Dolly. A man appeared dressed in a navy uniform, his dark hair slicked back. He smirked.

"Dolly, there's a dark-haired man here dressed in a navy uniform."

I opened my eyes and saw her shaking her head. She started waving her hands as if to swat a fly. Her upper lip was raised in disgust.

"He was a bastard. Is anyone else there? I'll take anyone but him."

I almost lost it. I took her hands again and closed my eyes.

"Dolly, now I have another male in spirit who wants to connect with you. He is showing me York, Maine. He's also holding up a bottle of Scotch."

Dolly shot up from the couch and put her hands on her hips.

"You've got to be kidding me! He made it to heaven?"

I tried to contain myself and bit my lip to not burst out into laughter.

Dolly started to gather her bag and umbrella.

"I came in to talk to my dead cat, not my shithead ex-husbands. Thanks anyway."

When ABC Media Productions filmed a presentation reel, which served as a "teaser" for cable networks interested in buying the show, we chose to do the reading at the Tirrell Room in Quincy, Massachusetts, for its breathtaking views of the Blue Hills. The Blue Hills were named by early European explorers who, while sailing along the coastline, noticed the bluish hue on the slopes when viewed from a distance. The bluish color comes from the presence of the mineral riebeckite in the stone along the hills.

I walked by a young woman and heard someone shouting in my head, "She's my daughter. Stop!"

"Is your father passed?" I asked her.

"Oh my God, yes!" she squealed.

I asked her to come up to the dance floor to make the connection to her dad. Her mom, uncle, and sisters followed her up.

"Dad is talking about a wedding."

The entire group gasped and burst into tears. The young woman I first went to spoke first.

"I got married a month ago, and my dad passed two weeks before my wedding."

Her dad showed me familiar scenes in my own database of Aruba, including the Divi Divi resort.

"So, you stayed at the Divi Divi for your honeymoon?"

The shrieks got louder.

"I can't believe this is happening. My dad presented me with an all-expense paid trip to the Divi Divi for our honeymoon." She grabbed her husband's hand.

"Well, just so you know, he went with you."

There was an awkward pause as they all looked at one another. Mom grabbed the microphone. "That's great because the entire family went on the honeymoon."

Dad told me that his daughter was expecting a baby boy. I wasn't sure if it was cool to relay this to her. She was quite petite and certainly didn't look pregnant.

"Dad is showing me a new baby."

They all looked at one another perplexed.

"No, I'm not pregnant," the new bride exclaimed.

"We plan to wait five years."

"Well," I said. "There's a CVS drugstore up the street. You might want to grab a stick."

She and her fiancé giggled. I was *dead* serious. She wrote to me a week later to let me know she took a test "for the heck of it" and was indeed pregnant!

Six years ago I gave a reading to a woman named Sue, in her fifties, who had just lost her dad. She took care of him and felt completely distraught at losing him. She hoped to find out if he was okay after passing. Dad was a very strong man of Italian descent. It didn't take him long to make the connection.

"Your dad is here. He's showing me he had colon cancer or cancer deep in the belly. I feel like my ass is falling out."

Sue looked surprised but happy.

"Is he okay? Is he happy with everything I tried to do for him? Does he know how much I miss him?"

"Yes, he's very happy. He's out of pain and still has a great sense of humor. He knows how much you miss him. He's smiling so big. He says the money is under the stairs."

We both laughed, and Sue seemed relieved. I went on to tell her many facts about her dad's life here on earth. He showed me that he built houses and cut his thumb off. She left feeling lighter.

I ran into Sue about two months after the reading while grocery shopping. She came toward me looking upset.

"Maureen, there was no money under the stairs. We had an excavator come in a week after our reading and they found nothing. Can you ask my father again where the money is?"

I was flabbergasted. I had no words. After I gathered myself and took a deep breath, I explained that when dad said, "The money is under the stairs," he was kidding.

I'm blessed to be known for my mediumship throughout New England, but sometimes being recognized is not as exciting as it sounds. Simple things like buying groceries at times turn into whispers and stares. In the produce section of my local supermarket one day I kept hearing a "psssst" sound coming from the lettuce section. A middle-aged woman pretended to look for lettuce, while she tried to get my attention. I finally looked over and she whispered, "Is my brother here? He just died."

I said, "No, he's over in the deli section. I'm busy looking for a good head of romaine."

You guessed it: she bolted to try to catch him before he left.

I recently taught a class on spirit communication. I firmly believe everyone can connect to their own loved ones in spirit. As we welcomed everyone into the classroom, one woman looked familiar.

"Where do I know you from? You look so familiar."

Instead of speaking, she took her hands, formed a box in front of her chest, and made a squishing gesture.

"I did your mammogram," she proudly exclaimed. "Everyone in the office freaked out when they saw you coming in."

"So, did they fight over who would assist me?"

"Ahh, not exactly. Nobody wanted to do it. They were all afraid you would bring through dead people during the procedure."

This sparked a memory from the year before during my very first mammogram. If you have not had the pleasure of experiencing book-ends crushing your breast, imagine a vise pressing your soft, sensitive skin into a very thin pizza crust.

Last year, midcrush, turned to the side, left breast served up on a plat-ter of Plexiglas, as the backhoe beeping sound echoed in the room, the "mammo operator" asked me to hold my breath. I took a deep breath in, praying to anyone that would listen for this to be over quickly. The operator said, "Is my father saying anything to you right now?"

Really? Are you kidding me! Do you think my nipples are some sort of antennae to heaven? Actually, yes, he is telling you to release the Vulcan death grip on my left breast. I can't wait for my next pap smear.

I do sometimes allow spirit to come through when I'm not "work-ing." Spirits love to get my attention while I'm out at a restaurant. (I like to call it "dinner and drinks with the dead.") I have to work hard to keep them quiet, especially when I'm ordering my meal. I was with a few of my sisters at Dave's Diner, a local 1950s-style restaurant.

The waitress's sister in spirit would not leave me alone. Finally, I broke down and made the connection.

"I've got this woman here in spirit who refuses to let me eat. She says she's your sister."

The waitress dropped a pile of menus and froze on the spot. She sat down next to me, drained by grief, and wept quietly.

"Your sister had breast cancer," I said. She is showing me a big "C" and I feel pressure in the front of my chest. Does she have three kids? She's holding up three fingers."

"Oh my God, first of all, she did have breast cancer and she has three kids."

I said, "She wants to thank you for taking such good care of her and now, her kids."

At this point, the waitress sobbed uncontrollably. Many of the patrons stared at us. They must have thought our eggs were overcooked and we weren't having it. Later, after my impromptu morning of coffee, doughnuts, and the dead, I got up and went over to hug the waitress.

I've done many unexpected readings at various places, such as clothing stores at the mall, my dentist's office, bars, bookstores, flower shops, my ophthalmologist's office, public restrooms, sporting events, hospitals, a commuter train, and, one, during a spray-tan session.

Recently, a friend on Facebook, Kathleen Gallagher Perry, shared an experience that is beyond priceless. My cheeks hurt from laughing after reading her story:

Funny story . . . I was teaching second-grade CCD today. Here was the conversation:

Little girl: "Mrs. Perry, how come there are only pictures of Jesus and no pictures of God in this book?

Mrs. Perry: "Well, God is everywhere. You really can't see him like people could see Jesus."

Little girl: "I bet Maureen Hancock could see him."

Laughter is the best medicine. If I can help those left behind to laugh through their pain, then I've done my job. So, go ahead and allow yourself a good laugh, perhaps after a good cry. Embrace all the days of your lives so you can be proud of the years between the dash on your headstone.

Here is a simple grounding exercise that will help when you feel out of sorts and unbalanced. Envision yourself standing in the middle of a field. Take a breath and imagine the roots of a tree, filled with the energy of the earth, coming up from the bottoms of your feet. The roots are gently wrapping around your legs and supporting you. You are firmly planted yet flexible. Now imagine a white ball of light at your feet. Imagine this warm, glowing protective light slowly moving up your legs, through your torso, neck, and head. Imagine it permeating your entire body. This is your white-light protection or energy blanket. It acts as a force field protecting you from negative energy. Now get out there and laugh, cry, and heal.

Conclusion

I've spent the past four years shaping my first book—my dream is now a reality. Starting out, I hoped this book would help you laugh, cry, and understand death as you joined me in my adventures as a real-life ghost whisperer. I now realize this book is so much more than just reading someone else's story. It's a culmination of stories from tragedy to triumph. It's a guidebook on transitioning from life to death and back again, and on living life to the fullest in memory of our loved ones in spirit. Mostly, I hope this book helps you become more divinely aware and opens your intuition like a flower whose seed was planted and just needed nurturing. Perhaps you will even be inspired to reach for the stars, believing all things are possible.

We are all given the incredible gift of life. How we choose to live it is the true gift. Do you shrink back at the mere thought of moving through grief, transitions, and life changes? Or do you allow yourself to feel the pain—thereby letting the healing begin? Some of the parents I've sat with who have physically lost children spend much of their time waiting and focusing on the ultimate reunion beyond. In this space, they find a way to go on—no longer fearing death but welcoming it. To my sister Rosie's credit, she does not spend her life waiting for death. Even though we discuss how glorious it will be when she gets to see Sean again, she has made a pact with him to live this magnificent adventure called life and make him proud. (After all, he is on his own adventure). Death has not removed her passion for life. Living life in this moment has brought her closer to Sean.

Death is the biggest mystery and most profound experience each of us will have in this lifetime. My deep-down desire is that by joining me on this journey, you not only learn to understand life after death, but how to *live*—not just living as in getting up each day, going to work, and doing it all over again the next day. But living with joy. Squeeze bits of joy out of each day until all those bits explode around you like confetti. Those on the other side want this for you. They root for you to gain understanding and clarity about death, dying, and the afterlife.

As I grow and learn from each experience, I continue to feel profoundly moved by the parents I meet who have had to say their physical good-byes to a child, and to those who never got a chance to say good-bye. When my energy reserves are low and I need to give healing messages to a crowd, I call in some of my young helpers—Sean Michael, Nick, Jennifer, D.J., Jonathan, Bo, Anjuli, Drew, and Maddie. They stand in my mind's eye holding hands and smiling, ready to assist another child give messages of hope and healing to their parents who sit anxiously in my audience.

I may be the "Medium Next Door," but I'm no different from you. We all have the ability to hear, feel, and see our loved ones in spirit. I hope you now have a deeper understanding of spirit communication and have learned how to quiet your mind, trust, and listen. When you do, the layers of grief might just start to peel away.

As I stand on the verge of spreading my message across the nation through my own television show—something I only dreamed of happening—I know God, my angels, and my special loved ones in spirit cleared the way for me to spread my message globally. I hope "my message" becomes your message—and that we can help others to stop fearing death and to understand the physical loss of a loved one in a new, enlightened way. If something resonates in your heart from this story, please share it with your family and friends.

*I believe that imagination is stronger than knowledge—
myth is more potent than history. I believe that
dreams are more powerful than facts—hope always triumphs over
experience—laughter is the only cure for grief.
And I believe that love is stronger than death.*

—Robert Fulghum

Appendix:
Frequently Asked Questions

Many people have questions about the afterlife, spirit communication, and spirituality in general. I'm constantly called upon to answer these questions during a demonstration, through the many e-mails I receive, or when I'm just hanging out at the ball field with my boys. These answers have been gathered through the experiences I've had in my work and what spirit tells me. Some of these answers are simply my opinion and will be verified when I get to the other side.

Q: What is a spirit medium?

A: A spirit medium is a person who communicates with spirits telepathically by hearing, feeling, and seeing visual impressions, symbols, and scenes from the spirit world or heaven. A medium is able to receive and connect with the higher frequencies or energies that our loved ones in spirit vibrate with. For me, the messages come in my own voice but are the thoughts and impressions of your loved one in spirit. It's like a stadium filled with people, or better yet, similar to the Verizon commercial where "the network" (a large crowd) shows up at a customer's door.

It is my interpretation of this fast-moving information and images that is transmitted to the recipient in a reading. My translation can be a little off at times but usually, about 90 percent of the information makes sense at the time of a session, and there's a good chance any information not understood at that time will make sense later. Names of the living and of those past are always brought up in a reading. Your loved ones on the other side like to acknowledge who they are, who they are with, and who they have left behind. They don't show up holding a sign saying, "I'm Billy, forty-two years old, a Gemini, and I enjoy long walks on the beach." If I had a nickel for every time someone asks if spirits give lottery numbers, I'd have a lot of nickels. Oh, and forget pennies from heaven. I'm still waiting for silver dollars!

Q: Does everyone have the ability to communicate with spirits?

A: Yes, everyone has a God-given gift of intuition and the ability to receive messages. Some people are more open to this ability. Like any ability, such as playing a musical instrument, some people are naturals and some need more practice. Tools such as meditation, yoga, spiritual books, listening to development tapes for building psychic abilities, and learning how to tune out mind chatter are just a few ways to tap into your own intuitiveness. Have you ever thought of someone and almost immediately the phone rings or you bump into them? If the answer is yes, then guess what . . . you're a bit psychic! If you *physically* bump into them, you're just a tad psychotic (just kidding!). Now, learn not to fear your ability, but trust it, let go, and watch as this ability helps guide you and your family for years to come. Sounds easy, huh? It takes practice.

Q: **Isn't mediumship against the Catholic Church and Christian teachings?**

A: On occasion, while in a session, a client might say their mother or father wouldn't come through because it's against their religion. I myself was raised Irish Catholic and I'm still Irish and Catholic. My faith allows me to deliver messages of hope, peace, and unconditional love from the higher side of life. I see nothing but beautiful healing occur after a connection to heaven—and that's anything but evil. To quote St. Paul about the gifts of the Holy Spirit: "There are diversities of gifts, but the same Spirit . . . But the manifestation of the Spirit is given to each one for the profit of all: for to one is given the word of wisdom through the Spirit, to another the word of knowledge through the same Spirit, to another faith by the same Spirit, to another gifts of healings by the same Spirit, to another the working of miracles, to another prophecy, to another discerning of spirits, to another different kinds of tongues, to another the interpretation of tongues. But one and the same Spirit works all these things, distributing to each one individually as He wills." (1 Cor. 12:4–11)."

I believe the Lord gives each of us special gifts through the holy spirit. These gifts are bestowed in many forms. Mediumship is the gift of prophecy. Throughout the Old and the New Testaments, God has always communicated to his people through mediumship. This communication manifested through many forms; angels, visions, the so-called dead, or dreams. The birth of Jesus and John the Baptist were prophesized. John the Baptist prophesized the coming of the Messiah (John 1:6–9). Mediumship is acknowledged through "supernatural" and "miraculous" happenings, upon which most, if not all, Christian teachings are based. God is present and active in all my gifts.

Q: **How can I communicate with my loved ones in heaven?**

A: You already do when you think of them. Your thoughts go directly to them and they hear you clearly. All you need is to be patient, willing, and not fearful. Forcing it won't help. I often sit with parents who have lost children and many of them say it's hard to get signs. I help to point out the very subtle ones, such as waking up between 3:00 and 4:00 AM, when the veil is thinnest between this side and the other side. And things such as driving in the car and not really listening to the words of a song when suddenly the words hit you and mean something special. There are many ways our loved ones send us messages and communicate. We just need to learn how to differentiate between our own thoughts and theirs.

How many of you have been driving and heard a voice in your head telling you to turn around? Much to your surprise, a truck or another vehicle is about to slam into your car and you experience a near miss. Now, if you hadn't turned around, you might be visiting your local auto body shop. Our loved ones guide us and the bond of love is not cut because the physical shell is gone. Our spirits are eternal and live way beyond the life of the used car we call our bodies.

Q: Are you hearing dead people all the time? How do you shut it off?

A: When I first realized I had this ability, I didn't have much control over it. My friend Tom Frederick, a Native American shaman, helped me realize that I was in control and I could turn the switch on and off. He said I was too open and overly empathic, causing the spirits to think they could come to me anytime they wanted. Once I realized that it was up to me, the spirits stopped hounding me and poking their heads out of my closet. (Although that was sometimes fun, especially when I was just falling asleep and I'd hear: "Hey, Maureen, it's me, Bob. You're reading my daughter tomorrow. Just thought I'd poke in to say hi."

Now, I can pretty much sleep through the night. Though, if I do a big event, I might be woken up by some renegade spirits who couldn't get through and have no "spirit etiquette."

Q: Is there a heaven and hell?

A: I would need a separate book just to answer this question. Throughout the ages, various religions reference heaven and hell in their teachings. My own personal opinion is that we create our own realities. I don't believe in an actual place called hell where fire and brimstone light up the night and a man in a red suit with horns and a tail is waiting at the gates. God gave us a special gift called "free will." I believe there are different levels of heaven, depending on how we lived out our earthly existence. I also believe that there are lower vibrating levels where spirits exist who were badly behaved (to put it lightly). Those in spirit who strived to live the spiritual laws of success such as loving unconditionally, helping others, being nonjudgmental, and not getting caught up in material things, have a much higher vibration around them and seem closer to God. Again, I am not God. Ultimately, I will find out the answers with the rest of you.

Q: Are there "bad" spirits?

A: There are lower vibration spirits that can be mischievous and sometimes unsettling. Personally, I protect myself with prayer. I put up boundaries around me and surround myself with the light of God. These lower energies feed on fear, so it's important to know you are in control. If you experience an unwanted energy, which may give you goose bumps or a nauseous feeling in your stomach, tell it to leave and mean it. Holding the covers over your head and whimpering will not help. Speak to them by saying, "I'll pray for you, but you have to leave now. Go to the light." Say it with conviction and try not to get caught up in the anxious feeling you have. Try not to let fear take over and create the false energy of a bad spirit. Our minds are powerful tools and can sometimes cause undue worry and stress.

On a similar note, I am not a fan of Ouija boards. They bring in unwanted energies that sometimes don't leave. I'm even more leery of children and teens playing around with a board. My friend Nancy was a teen when she experimented with a Ouija board. When she went to bed, it felt like something was sitting on her chest. It took a few weeks for this feeling to go away. The board is not a toy—stay away from it.

If you notice a mischievous energy in your home, particularly in a child's room, try using sage or sweetgrass for smudging. Dried sage bundles and sweetgrass—which can be found in holistic stores or Native American shops—are a Native American tradition used for cleansing and purifying an area. Light one end of the bundle and wave the smoke around an area.

I had luck dealing with a mischievous energy in my children's room by hanging a Native American dream catcher by the window. For added protection, hang a religious cross somewhere in the room and sprinkle holy water around. As parents, we want to protect our children. Talk to the energy that is being mischievous or possibly causing your child to be uncomfortable. Tell them they are scaring your child and that they have to leave.

Q: **What happens when we go to heaven?**

A: From what spirits tell me, they go through what is called an "orientation." It's a tour of heaven for a newly arrived spirit. They reunite with loved ones and get to see their spirit guide and other guides again. If a spirit is having a hard time adjusting, the other spirits assist like a social worker or therapist would for the living. They also get to review their Book of Life, in which they examine what they have done in regards to thoughts, words, and deeds while on earth. From there, some take a rest, have celebrations, sometimes spend time alone. Some study, some work, and some heal from their physical death or leaving a loved one behind. The spirits and we are all the same in many ways, yet different when it comes to dealing, coping, and handling certain things like feelings, choices, and free will.

Q: What does heaven look like?

A: What I have seen with spirits is that each of them has their own "version" of heaven (something like a screen saver). They create their heaven to be whatever they feel comfortable with. For instance, a spirit might show me that they are sitting by the ocean, just as they loved to do here. Or they might show themselves to me in a way that is familiar to the loved one I am speaking with—fishing, boating, hiking in the mountains, or working on the farm they grew up on.

Q: Are my loved ones in heaven still angry with me?

A: I have not come across any spirit who is angry with their loved ones, even if there was a problem between the two people. Each spirit has come through to me with nothing but unconditional love. The reason for this is that in heaven you get to see the bigger picture of what your life was here and all who were in it. Also, God is nothing but pure unconditional love and forgiveness, and so spirits love and forgive, too. Many times, they tell me to tell their loved one to forgive themselves so that they, spirits, *and* the living can live life more fully. Have faith that all the crap is left here.

Q: Do animals communicate with messages from heaven?

A: Animals absolutely communicate in much the same way as human spirits. I have personally experienced it numerous times when I've connected clients to their animals beyond. Amazingly, the animal speaks to me in a very human way, and their messages are just the same as human messages.

Q: **Are animals sensitive to a spirit's energy?**

A: In general, animals, especially dogs, are very sensitive to energy in the room. They may bark and appear as though they are looking at something or someone, and nobody is there. Cats appear more agitated when a spirit is in the room. They might be extra vocal and go over to the area where the energy is.

Q: **How do you communicate with the spirits of people who did not speak English?**

A: Language is universal in heaven. Spirits communicate in my language so that I can understand them. The same goes for infants and animals. Sometimes, though, if some phrase has special significance, the spirit will communicate it to me in his or her native language. For instance, I was once doing a reading for a Greek woman. Her husband was coming through, and my friend, Maryanne, who is fluent in Greek, was interpreting my words. However, the husband kept on repeating the same thing over and over to me in Greek and I kept repeating what I was hearing: *Ska'se Malaka*. Maryanne was kicking me under the table, but the woman was smiling and nodding. She seemed quite happy with the message, so I didn't understand the daggers my friend was sending me.

Finally, I whispered to her, "What is he saying?"

Maryanne gritted her teeth and whispered under her breath, "Shut up, idiot!"

I let out a gasp, but the old Greek woman grabbed my hand and said in broken English, "Now I know it is him. He always said that to me!"

Acknowledgments

It would take me half the book to thank those that helped this vision become a reality. So many friends and family members have supported me during the process of sharing my messages through this book and television. Here are just a handful of people who have paved the way and held me up. Thank you to:

My immediate family—Greg, Tyler, and Drew, my earth angels, for your patience, unconditional love, and support.

The Dalton Gang—Mom, Dad, Rosie, Jim, Liz, Maggie, Joe, Marygrace, Sarah, and Patrice. You are all the wind beneath my wings.

Anastassia Grace and Candy Dalton—love and thanks to my beautiful, gifted nieces.

Lisa Tener—my incredibly gifted book coach and friend. I am deeply grateful for your guidance and expertise. I could not have done this without you.

Imal Wagner—my friend and literary agent. Thank you for lighting the way and helping me believe dreams can come true.

Carol Rosenberg—my amazing editor at HCI Books. Words are inadequate to express my gratitude for the patience, energy, and remarkable skill you poured into this book.

Peter Vegso—founder, HCI Books. Thank you for taking a chance on me and helping a dream come true.

Nancy Burke—Thank you for sprinkling your outstanding editing talent throughout this book.

Marianne Leone Cooper (and Jesse)—my dear friend and guide. Thank you for your unwavering support, sharing your talents, and helping me find my voice.

Dot Aufiero—without your tireless efforts and belief in me, I would not be where I am today.

Kelly Scriven—a special thank you to my friend and manager. I'm deeply grateful for your unending belief in me and holding the torch through this marathon.

Wanda McManus—my dear friend and assistant. Thank you for keeping me strong and organized!

Sandy Alemian—I count you among my treasures. Thank you for your guidance, support, and unconditional love.

Kerry Brett—my soul sister and amazing photographer. Thank you for bringing *The Medium Next Door* to life.

Larry Quemere—a special thank-you for always looking out for me and providing a sacred space for healing to the masses.

I'd like to give special thanks to some of my closest friends for their unending support and encouragement: Lori Belche, Maryann Georgantas, Diane, Katie, Melissa and Erica Laubi, the Fontneaus, Ellie

Bassick-Trovato and the Uplifting Connections staff, John Holland, Noelle Armstrong, Jaqi Murphy, Paula Wonson, Lisa Hockney, Lorna Brunelle, Ted Lopes, Shelley Hines, John Trifiro, Teesha Latec, Kendall and Dina Fisher, Father Al Faretra, the Bridgewater Badger moms, and Juliana Fehrer.

To my friends in television and media—thank you for your belief and faith in me: Elaine Metaxas, Rebecca Eisen (my soul sister), David Stone, Anne Lewis Roberts (and all the staff at ABC Media Productions), Kim Moses and Ian Sander (Sander/Moses Productions), Stephen Brown (20th Century Fox Television), Cal Boyington, Dan Ilani, Steve Wohl at Paradigm Talent Agency, the executives at Style. Thank you for seeing the vision. I look forward to the journey.

J. R. Reitz, Michael Rock, and Larry Soares at Fun 107 radio, Loren and Wally and the entire team at WROR radio, Eric Latek at Phantazma Pictures, and John Belche at Outsource Creations.

To my special friends who contributed to the book with their heartfelt stories—Rosie Dalton, Dave Kane and Joanne O'Neill, Suzanne D'Olimpio Falco, Gail Hunter, Mary Rizzo, Madison Armstrong, Donna Wells, Julie and Pete Ostiguy, and Kristen Savoie.

Detective Alan Tate and the team at Metro Investigations—our passion to help bring the children home has only just begun in our joint effort, "Mission for the Missing." Thank you for always being there for me.

Detective Cindy Felts and Chief John LaCrosse.

And to all those who are reading this and feel left out: I am blessed to have an abundance of friends who help me in many areas of my life. Thank you.

Resources

Bereaved Parents of the USA

www.bereavedparentsusa.org

A nationwide organization designed to aid and support bereaved parents and their families struggling to overcome their grief after the passing of a child.

Compassionate Friends

www.compassionatefriends.org

A nationwide organization of bereaved parents offering friendship, support groups and one-on-one assistance in your area.

Forever Family Foundation

www.foreverfamilyfoundation.org

To further the understanding of Afterlife Science through research and education while providing support and healing for people in grief.

Wings

www.wingsgrief.org

Information and inspiration for the bereaved and caregivers, including a quarterly magazine of real stories about people's journeys through grief.

Books

The Care and Feeding of Indigo Children by Doreen Virtue

Comfort: A Journey Through Grief by Ann Hood

The Complete Idiot's Guide to Communicating with Spirits by
    Rita Berkowitz and Deborah S. Romaine

Healing Grief: Reclaiming Life After Any Loss by James Van Praagh

Jesse: A Mother's Story of Grief, Grace, and Everday Bliss by
    Marianne Leone

Soul Shift: Finding Where the Dead Go by Mark Ireland

We Are Eternal: What the Spirits Tell Me About Life After Death by
    Robert Brown

What Was God Thinking?! I Wanted to Know . . . So I Asked by
    Sandy Alemian

About the Author

Maureen Hancock is a nationally renowned spirit medium, teacher, lecturer, and holistic healer, and has spent the last ten years using her abilities to give back. She is cofounder of two nonprofit organizations: Seeds of Hope, holistic care for cancer patients and support for parents who have lost children, and Mission for the Missing, which provides assistance and equipment in missing children and adult cases. Maureen is an associate member of the Licensed Private Detective Association of Massachusetts. She has been featured in numerous articles and can be heard on radio stations around the country. Additionally, Maureen has appeared on the Fox talk show *Wedlock or Deadlock* and is currently developing her own reality television show with ABC/Disney and the executive producers of *The Ghost Whisperer*, Sander/Moses Productions. Maureen resides in a small town south of Boston, Massachusetts, with her husband, two children, and chocolate lab, Ally.

For further information about Maureen, her appearance calendar, or to subscribe to her free e-mail newsletter, visit: www.maureenhancock.com. Also visit www.seedsofhope.com and www.missionforthemissing.com.